Royal Boro
Greenw
Coldhart
William Barefo
020 8857 7346

D0431508

10|13
Wo: 20-1-18

Thank you!

To renew, please contact any Royal
Greenwich library or renew online at
www.royalgreenwich.gov.uk/libraries

GREENWICH LIBRARIES

3 8028 02104787 0

The
Accidental
Carer

100 tips for meeting the challenges
when caring for a stroke survivor

Nicole Banerji

Copyright © 2009 Nicole Banerji

The moral right of the author has been asserted.

Apart from any fair dealing for the purposes of research or private study,
or criticism or review, as permitted under the Copyright, Designs and Patents
Act 1988, this publication may only be reproduced, stored or transmitted, in
any form or by any means, with the prior permission in writing of the
publishers, or in the case of reprographic reproduction in accordance with
the terms of licences issued by the Copyright Licensing Agency. Enquiries
concerning reproduction outside those terms should be sent to the publishers.

Matador
5 Weir Road
Kibworth
Leicester
LE8 0LQ
Email: books@troubador.co.uk
Web: www.troubador.co.uk/matador

ISBN9781848762114

Typeset in 11pt Verdana by Troubador Publishing Ltd, Leicester, UK

Matador is an imprint of Troubador Publishing Ltd

Printed in Great Britain by the MPG Books Group, Bodmin and King's Lynn

*For Dad, who smiled when I started
this book, urging me to call it
'My Poor Old Dad'.*

GREENWICH LIBRARIES	
CO	
3 8028 02104787 0	
Askews & Holts	27-Sep-2013
920 BANE	£8.99
4044109	

Acknowledgements

Heartfelt thanks to all those who were there
for Dad and I, supporting us on our journey into the
unknown.

Special mention to Alex, Ruchira, Brenda, Brian,
Colin and Zoe.

Contents

Prologue

The Whirlwind Begins

22nd March 2006

What a day it had been. Travelling back on the evening train from London I felt a warm satisfaction with life. The official launch of our research report on university admissions had gone off without a hitch. The Minister had turned up and done his bit, so had the Press. The workshop sessions had gone well and we had generated lots of interest in our findings. That rosy glow was like sinking into a warm bubble bath. It was all the more welcome as no-one could have said that this project had been stress free. Oh no, but that's another story. But now my part in it was over and I could relax and turn my attention to trying to get a bit of free publicity from the local Press for my up and coming book signing next week. Surely someone would be interested in my first book, *How to Gossip*?

I started to think about my life. A sense of warm satisfaction descended as I opened my second mini bottle of Virgin Train wine. I felt contented, things had worked out pretty well. Since deciding to leave the hurly burly of consultancy a few years ago I had managed to carve out a busy, fulfilling way of living. I was managing to do enough freelance consultancy work as a psychologist to fuel my champagne (well maybe cava) lifestyle, but with no intention whatsoever in building my own business. My friends liked to brand this as 'psycho-tarting'. This worked out as having to find about 5 days a month of real work, leaving loads of time to do other things. These other things tapped into my more creative side. I had started a little textile design business, had made no money whatsoever, but I loved it. I had also recently been inspired to start writing. The first book, a little whimsy on Gossip, was starting to sell and maybe my forthcoming interview on a Canadian talk radio station would stimulate a few international sales. I decided that I must really sort out a proper marketing strategy the following week. I had no excuses now that the big project was over.

I got in about 10.30pm. Saw the message from Alex that he had popped to the pub with an old school friend and that there was some of his extra hot 20 chilli curry left over if I wanted a thrill. Bless. Toddled up the stairs to the office to see what was waiting for me on the email system. My ansaphone was flashing, I was Mrs Popularity and had 2 messages. I pressed play whilst turning on the computer and starting to unpack my briefcase.

"*I was wondering if you sell crepe paper? If you do could you ring me back on 0161 766 8898*"

It must have been the fifth call this week from someone thinking that I was a craft shop rather than a textile artist. Sigh. Still, it shows that there is room for a shop of this kind in the area if I ever fancy another change of career.

"*Uh hello, it's Sarah. Your father is in hospital. He fell down the stairs and has a broken finger. They think that he may have had a slight stroke. Bye then.*"

Aha, short and direct, as Sarah's messages always were. She was my Dad's (ex) ladyfriend (?). Heaven knows what the status of their friendship was. They met 7 years ago, a couple of years after my Mum died. My Dad went from being sad and lonely to being totally infatuated in a couple of months, and it wasn't long before she had moved into his bungalow, despite having a house of her own in a neighbouring village. These pensioners certainly know how to live the rock and roll lifestyle! Dad's friends were always voicing concerns about her motives, but my view was, if she makes him happy what the heck! She lived with him for a couple of years before moving out to go and live 100 miles away to be nearer to her grandchildren. Although Dad was not happy about this development, they still saw each other fairly frequently. Dad had been staying with her for a couple of weeks.

Should I ring her back? It was quite late, and from her message it didn't sound too bad. A broken finger? A slight stroke? No I would ring tomorrow morning to see what was what.

Challenge One

Getting Information
out of the Professionals

Dad's story

A slight stroke was a touch of an understatement.

In reality Dad was experiencing a massive trauma to the right side of his brain which was confirmed a week later when he eventually had a scan. The hospital seemed to focus more on the effects of the tumble down the stairs than the sneaky little stroke that had prompted the misfooting. Everything grinded slowly, there was little sign of the immediate diagnoses and urgent test taking we are used to seeing in Holby City!

Dad was in hospital for 3 months, with the first 6 weeks of this being on a male general medical ward. The hospital was 100 miles away from where I lived, and thus started a pattern of visiting which with hindsight was exhausting, but at the time seemed perfectly feasible, I was on automatic. Three times a week, I would leave home at 1.00 in the afternoon and trundle up the M6 in my little car. I'd get there at 3.00, the start of visiting time, and leave at 5.00, getting home in time for Coronation Street. All this whilst juggling my freelance work and imminent book launch. Thank goodness that I worked for myself, I don't know what would have happened if I had not had the freedom to manage my own diary.

Dad was very ill. His stroke had totally paralysed his left side leaving him unable to walk, unable to use the toilet and even unable to get himself into a more comfortable position when in bed. He was also uncommunicative, in pain from the tumble down the stairs, depressed and very drowsy. When he was awake he would constantly shout for the nurses. They had got used to this and ignored it, coming only when they needed to attend to him. This lack of attention made him even more frustrated and so he would shout even louder! At under 9 stone, Dad had always been a slight man, but during his 6 weeks on Ward 101 he managed to lose a further 2 stone. No-one was ensuring that he actually ate the food that was put out for him. In his weakened, malnourished state he also picked up several infections and had several little fits. He appeared to be on an ever downward spiral. We were all very worried.

During this time, surprisingly little information was freely given to us about Dad's condition and his prognosis. Doctor's rounds were in the morning and all those treating my Dad had well and truly left the building by the time visiting time started at 3.00. Whenever I enquired at the Nurses Station as to how my Dad had been I got a variety of statements that didn't really answer my fundamental but unspoken questions:

> "not too bad, about the same"
> "he ate his dinner today"
> "the doctor has increased his painkillers"

The only pieces of useful information were the notes left by Barbara, his Stroke Worker. Until the first note appeared in the third week I was totally unaware that she was seeing Dad. She would come and work with him 3 – 4 times a week and was the only member of hospital staff that he had formed a relationship with and was cooperative with. She left a notepad on Dad's locker and after each session she would write half a page detailing what they had tried to do. Dad's progress and achievements were jotted down, as was his frame of mind and her predictions as to when he could be ready to go to the hospital's specialist rehabilitation unit. It was amazing how much difference these notes made to me. They gave me some real hope that Dad would actually get out of Ward 101 alive! This was the start of an enduring friendship that would last beyond Dad's time in hospital.

Transferring to the rehabilitation unit became a bone of contention. As the weeks went by it was clear that Dad was not regaining any movement in those paralysed limbs. As he lay there broken and depressed in his hospital bed with his face to the wall, I would see other men with strokes come into the ward and get transferred to rehab within days. They did not appear to be doing significantly better than Dad in regaining their functions, I couldn't understand it. When I started asking as to when Dad could go to rehab I got different answers depending on who I asked. The problem seemed to be that Dad was 'inconsistent in how much he would try to do things/cooperate'. Hardly surprising when one's life has been totally ripped apart.

Barbara was positive and thought he was ready to go there after 3 weeks, that he was only waiting for a bed to become available.

The Staff Nurse thought that he would not be able to take advantage of rehab due to his 'lack of positive attitude' and as he had not got to rehab within 2 weeks it was likely that he would go straight from the ward to nursing care. She let slip that Dad's case had been discussed with the rehab staff and that they had refused to take him as he was 'difficult'.

The Consultant was more flexible. He was happy for Dad to go to rehab even though he was 'out of the normal time window', but he would have to wait until he had shaken off the infections he had picked up on the ward and was medically stable.

Even the hospital Social Worker had a take on this. He was under the impression that Dad had been offered a place in rehab but he had refused to go!

All this confusion and miscommunication was doing my head in. After Dad had been on Ward 101 for 5 weeks, Sarah and I arranged an appointment with the Consultant to find out exactly what was happening. Sarah was surprisingly quiet at this meeting. She was finding Dad's illness very difficult to cope with. She was extremely angry, feeling that Dad was not being properly cared for. At the meeting we explored issues of loss of weight, drowsiness, lack of positive attitude as well as the move to rehab. This was the first proper discussion there had been about my Dad's condition and it was instigated by us. A few days after this meeting Dad went to rehab.

Making sense of it all

It seems to me that strokes come in three forms.

Forget about the technical nuances for a bit, forget about those mini-strokes which are a clear warning sign. Once someone has had a stroke that sends them to hospital in an ambulance with the sirens screaming and the lights flashing, the family and friends want to know which type it is. Is it:

A stroke that although initially devastating, sees many of the major functions that were knocked out returning within a couple of weeks. Although some effects may be life changing and long lasting, the person makes a relatively quick partial or complete recovery.

A stroke that is so traumatic that it leads to death. The patient may die quickly, never fully regaining consciousness. They may die more slowly in hospital, either by their bodily functions slowly shutting off as a direct result of their brain injury or as an indirect result, by them succumbing to the myriad of infections that stalk our hospitals waiting to pounce on the frail and infirm.

Or is it a stroke that doesn't kill you. But the carnage that it leaves behind has permanent and severely disabling effects. There is no significant recovery, overnight the person goes from an active, communicative individual to someone who may have lost the ability to walk, to talk, to eat etc. Although gradual improvements may occur over time, their life will never be anything like what it used to be.

My Dad's stroke fell into this final category. Of course nobody knew this at the time. That's the thing with strokes, it is difficult to predict the outcome, one can

only keep looking for signs of recovery and hoping.
In times like this the family and friends are naturally
ravenous for information, they need to know the
basics, they know nothing whatsoever about this
condition, they may even hold unwarranted
assumptions. They want to know: is their loved one
going to die? What exactly has happened to them? Are
they going to die? How is the condition affecting them?
Are they going to die? What course does the condition
usually take? Are they going to die? How are they doing
in comparison to others/the expected course of events?
Are they going to die? What are the treatment options?
Are they going to die? How will the treatment be
decided? Are they going to die? Are they going to die?

Unfortunately circumstances can conspire to make it
likely that none of these questions get answered
properly, ever. Let's face it:

There are no easy answers, for many conditions,
including strokes, it is a game of wait and see. The
doctors and nurses don't know if the patient will die.

Even if the signs are good there can be a reluctance to
commit to an answer, especially if the patient is elderly or
vulnerable in any other way. This may be because a
sudden downturn can happen at any time and the doctors
and nurses don't want to give false hope. They are also
aware that we are fast becoming a self serving litigious
society. Grieving relatives need to make sense of what
has happened, where there is no neat explanation they
will often look for someone to blame. What if staff have
predicted recovery and it all turns to dust? Will there be
complaints of neglect? Malpractice? Will they be sued?

Getting hold of someone to ask is difficult. Many visiting times are confined to specific times during the day. Times when the doctors are tied up elsewhere. Catching a doctor is difficult and spotting a Consultant is just about impossible.

Many wards are understaffed. This means that the nurses and care assistants have just too much to do. They have less time to form relationships with the patients and relatives, they have less time to find out what is happening with any particular patient whilst they have been off duty, they have less time to talk to relatives and bring them up to speed, and generally will only do so if specifically asked. Even where the 'named nurse' system is in place it is often not working as it should do.

Under-resourcing tends to increase stress and dissatisfaction amongst the staff. Empathy with relatives, proactive communication and sunny dispositions tend to fall off the end pretty quickly under these circumstances. Busy, distracted, grumpy people can be very difficult to approach for information, especially if you are scared of what the answers could be.

Many staff are temporary, short term contract staff or have just come onto the ward to help out. They may not know about your loved one's situation.

Patients can have several visitors from different parts of their life who will come at different times. This motley bunch of concerned people may not know each other, they may not like each other or communicate with each other. This means that the staff can get fed up with giving out similar information to different people several times in one day.

Considering the above it is hardly surprising that patients and relatives alike still feel that they are kept somewhat in the dark. Finding someone to ask can be difficult. Once found they may be busy and thus, although they will be highly professional in answering any questions asked, as far as they can, they are likely to be reluctant to properly explore and discuss the situation in any depth. The likelihood of the important, scary, unspoken questions being dealt with is slim.

Ten top tips

1. Prepare in advance the questions you would really like answers to. Even the ones you are scared of asking. Write them down. If you don't, you will never ask them.

2. Discuss your questions with family and friends. Those closely involved will be able to add the questions that they need answering to your list, those less involved will be less emotional and will be able to add the gamut of logical questions not uppermost in your mind in the initial stages.

3. Be proactive. Don't wait for the staff to come to chat with you. They don't know what you know already, they don't know what you want to know, your loved one is only one of many passing through their care.

4. Don't rely on catching people in the corridor, arrange a meeting to discuss your questions. In the initial stages this is likely to be with the Sister in charge of the ward. It doesn't have to be a formal meeting, but it is likely to be more fruitful with the benefit of a degree of preparation on both sides. Why not pop into the Nurses Station at the start of your visit and ask if it would be possible to have a few words after your visit, maybe in an hour's time? This gives you time to review your questions, adding anything that is currently playing on your or your loved one's mind. It also gives the Sister time to review the patient file.

5. After getting the initial information, allow time for any treatment regime to start working. Don't make a nuisance of yourself by expecting a full scale briefing every time you visit.

6. Many people make significant progress in the first couple of weeks. Following this is a good time to ask for an appointment to see the Consultant. This is likely to be a meeting away from the ward and arranged via the Consultant's Secretary. If things have moved quickly and recovery is evident, the questions you would like to ask are likely to be different to your initial questions. If no recovery is apparent a different set of questions come to mind. In both instances, prepare in advance.

7.   Remember that these meetings are not just an opportunity to ask questions, they are also a way in which the Consultant can gauge the family's view on the different types of treatment regime. Don't be shy in sharing what you would like to happen ... without making hysterical demands of course! There is rarely one simple course of action. Priorities and choices can be influenced by your requests, ideas and observations.

8.   If faced with conflicting information and agendas from different sources, be aware that the Consultant is still king (or queen). Many different professionals may be involved in your loved one's care, but at the end of the day it is the Consultant who makes the decisions and who takes responsibility. If things are not going as you would wish then it is wise to spend time influencing the Consultant, getting them on your side.

9.   Learn how to interpret the patient charts at the end of the bed. Useful information regarding ongoing measures can be gleaned such as blood pressure, injuries, food consumed, weight, painkillers taken etc.

10. Keep other interested parties up to date. A regular email round can serve to allay fears that magnify in the absence of any useful information. A version of Barbara's notepad

by the bedside can be a marvellous record of progress. The professionals caring for your loved one may not always find the time to fill it in, but each visitor certainly can. This helps people to get a broader picture of how someone is in themselves. If you always visit at the end of the day and you constantly find the patient asleep or in pain it is a tremendous relief to find out that earlier in the day they were perky and positive. Believe me.

Challenge Two

Dealing with the Emotions

My story

"Your father is in pain, he knows he is dying."

Sarah got into the habit of sending me such texts late at night. I found them strange and very upsetting. What purpose could they possibly serve?

I must admit that I am not a massively emotional person. Although I care deeply for those close to me, my thought processes tend to be dominated by rationality and logic, just like Mr Spock in Star Trek. I am one of those women who cry about once every 2 years and who don't really understand what other women are on about when they admit to being in tears a couple of times a week. What's that all about? I am fairly task focused and have a tendency, when faced with problems, to work to sort them out rather than worry about them. On one personality test I even came out as a man!

Sarah, on the other hand, is at the other end of the spectrum. Even before my Dad had his stroke she always seemed to be het up about something or other. She seemed to be in a semi-permanent state of unresolved anger and on several occasions she had been known to launch into an unprovoked verbal attack on some innocent, based purely on unfounded assumptions. I knew that she had had some bad experiences in her life and I guessed that a lot of her dodgy behaviour stemmed from these. We got on

OKish, I wouldn't say that we were bosom buddies, she always seemed to be envious of the way Dad and I got on – not quite sure why, I was hardly a threat to her. I found her hard work, but my view was that Dad was old enough and silly enough to choose his own friends.

My initial reaction to Dad's stroke was fear. Fear that my Dad would die. Fear that I wouldn't be able to cope with what was ahead. Fear of the unknown. Although these fears never properly disappeared, they were quickly superceded by my natural optimism. Many people get better from strokes, why wouldn't Dad be one of those? I could visualise him making a good recovery and returning to living independently. As it became clear that a speedy recovery was not on the cards, and when Dad's condition was hit by complication after complication, that good old problem solving mode kicked in. I started focusing on the issues one by one, searching for ways to overcome them.

Dad was very good at looking on the bleak side, he did self pity very well, he was not what you would call a natural positive thinker. I felt that it was obvious that the family's role was to help him to motivate himself to get better and to see that recovery was possible. In my mind the first big step was to get Dad to rehab where he would get daily physiotherapy, occupational therapy etc. This was exactly what he needed. Lying around in ward 101 was doing his state of mind no good at all. The only shining light was when Barbara, his Stroke Worker, came in, and that was not every day. He needed clear goals to work to and a team of people to work with him to help him achieve some progress. Once this started to happen I was convinced that his positive attitude would develop. My focus was single-mindedly on my Dad and what I could do to help him recover. I had no time for my own emotions, the public crying didn't start till weeks later, not till it was pretty certain that he would survive!

Sarah's reaction was much different. Her emotions were boiling up all over the place. The major components were anger, loss, and a rather disturbing self absorption. I started to receive daily texts and emails complaining about the hospital staff and the way Dad was being treated. I empathised with her concerns, I assumed that this was just her way of letting off steam in private.

What I had no idea about was that she was being difficult and offensive with the hospital staff whenever she visited. I only found out months later that during this time she had: accused staff of deliberately trying to starve Dad; verbally attacked a couple of physiotherapists so badly that the hospital had offered them counselling; threatened to sue the hospital. No wonder all the staff looked wary whenever I visited, they must have thought that Sarah spoke for me also. Dad being branded as a 'difficult patient' also started to make sense. Not only was he a difficult patient, he had a nightmare family as well!

When Dad finally moved to rehab I was delighted. His mood lifted a little and he was getting all the attention he needed. I couldn't understand why I got the strong feeling that Sarah wasn't happy about this. She never said so directly, but now that her concerns about the big stuff had been alleviated, she started a liturgy of whinging and ranting about small stuff:

"Why had I been contacted, and not her, when Dad had a bit of a slide out of his chair?"

(I was officially his next of kin).

"Why did she have to do his washing now that he had to wear day clothes, she was fed up of this, it was difficult, she did not have a tumble drier?"

(She lived 5 miles away, I lived 100 miles away, Ruchira my half sister lived in India. It was June, and a very sunny one at that – hanging out on the line would be fine. So much fuss was made of this that Barbara even offered to take some washing home to pop into her machine!).

"Why did other patients have 4 pillows and Dad only had 2. He couldn't get comfy, why are they denying him extra pillows?"

(Hospital shortages – just bring some in for him to use the way other families did).

All this whinging seemed bizarre to me. Surely she would want to do anything she could to help? Things were not perfect in rehab but they were a lot better than on ward 101. Dad was much better in himself, he was starting to eat more, he was not as drowsy, and he was less depressed. He was looking forward to a visit from Ruchira and her family who were coming all the way from India to cheer him up. Although it was becoming clear that he was not making the strides I had hoped for on his mobility, I was pretty certain that the danger period was over and that he was not about to drop dead overnight.

It was about this time that my emotions started to catch up with me. I had a period of a couple of weeks where anything would set me off. On one occasion Alex and I had gone to a Harvey Nichols shopping evening to partake of the free champagne and canapes. Towards the end of the evening I found that tears were streaming down my face in the middle of the hats and bags section. Even worse, I didn't care a jot! As my emotions went haywire I found it liberating, exhausting and actually very interesting. Some people must be like this all the time! I wondered what coping strategies they developed to help them manage their wayward feelings – I had none to draw upon. At this time I started having e-chats with Ruchira. We had only met a few times, and did not really know each other. The chats started as just a way of keeping her up to date with Dad's condition, but soon transmuted into mutual support.

Making sense of it all

We don't all deal with the shock of a sudden life changing catastrophe in the same way. Sarah and I had very different reactions to Dad's stroke. The stress of the stroke served to push our natural approaches to opposite extremes, making it very difficult for either of us to understand where the other was coming from. What has occurred to me since that time was that Sarah never had any hope whatsoever that my Dad would recover. Consciously or unconsciously she expected him to die, thus she felt that rehab was a waste of time.

I should have gained an inkling of this when she complained bitterly about the physiotherapy he was having. She felt it was tiring him out, leaving him too tired in the afternoons to spend any quality time with her. It should have become clear to me when she kept going on about him *"needing sanctuary rather than being made a public spectacle of"*. This latter related to the practice of patients sitting in the public area outside their rooms, rather than by themselves in their rooms, so that staff could keep an eye on them. It seemed that Sarah had written him off. She was waiting for him to die. How easy it is to forget that different people experience the same situation in very different ways. These are shaped by our expectations. If we expect a positive outcome we focus on and pick up on the positives, whereas if we expect the worst, we latch onto anything negative that serves to confirm our predictions.

Our expectations then go on to influence our behaviour. At the time I found Sarah's behaviour bizarre and totally counterproductive. Instead of a source of support she became yet another problem to be dealt with. I did not have the energy, I needed all of that to do the 200 mile round trip to see my Dad three times a week, to work to help him focus on being more positive and active in his own recovery, whilst juggling all the other demands of my hectic life. I should have addressed these issues with Sarah, but I didn't. I just continued to be outwardly calm, trying to be supportive with her, whilst being inwardly irritated by her attitude, I didn't need the hassle at this difficult time. Dad certainly didn't need two of his nearest and dearest squabbling between themselves. Looking back, if we had talked about her behaviour upfront, maybe events would have taken a different turn?

Ten top tips

1.   The emotional challenges you are faced with may not always be the ones you expect. I fully expected my Dad's emotional reaction to his stroke to be anger, grief, fear and depression. His life had changed dramatically 'in a stroke'. Who would be happy under these circumstances? I was slightly surprised at the severity of my own delayed reaction, it seemed to come out of the blue. But what really took me off guard was the need to deal with other people's emotional reactions. At a time when we should all be pulling together they served to add another straw to the camel's back.

2.   Remember, you are not the star in this drama, you are only a supporting actor. No matter what your own emotional state, your role is there to help your loved one get into

the best possible psychological state to be able to bounce back. Their positive attitude will make all the difference to how they progress and how they tackle the inevitable setbacks.

3. In helping the person find their motivation to recover make sure that you balance empathy with positivity. Empathy about the awfulness of what has happened, without any positivity, can lead to inadvertently encouraging the patient to wallow in self pity, without giving them a way out of the mire. On the other hand, positivity without empathy can be a denial of the patient's right to be hurt and angry, they need to deal with these feelings before being able to fully move on.

4. Find reasons to praise and reassure. It is likely that your loved one will not only be feeling anger, loss and despair at their predicament, they will also simultaneously experience a dramatic loss of confidence. The task of recovery can seem an impossible feat. They need to see that they can do it. If a fairly rapid improvement takes place in the first couple of weeks, keep reminding them of that and how well they are doing. If little sign of improvement occurs, set little tasks for them to achieve. Latch onto anything which has gone in the right direction and milk it mercilessly.

5. Don't be afraid to get competitive. With my

Dad this was difficult as all the other stroke patients sprinted to rehab whilst he crawled there slipping and falling every inch of the way. However, remember the tortoise and the hare? It was a quirky source of macabre comfort to him to hear that some of the sprinters had taken a downturn and some had not survived. No matter what the situation there will be some interpretation of it that can be positive!

6. Make use of the recovery stories of others. There are many inspiring stories out there. A good source is the Stroke Association website. Select a person who has something in common with your loved one and draw the parallels. Make sure they know that they can do it too.

7. Don't be surprised if your own emotions don't kick in straight away. Many of those close to people who have experienced a stroke report that shock, numbness and operating on automatic were part of their experience too. But rest assured, there will be a time when the emotions come flooding in. Don't be surprised, don't be apologetic, surf the tides and get to shore.

8. Share your emotions with friends, family and other key players in your loved one's life, and get them to share their emotions too. Initiating communication that goes beyond the factual about improvements/

setbacks/test results etc can serve to cement bonds, helping all concerned in supporting each other. It can help the interested parties to understand where others are coming from, and hopefully reduce the risk of misunderstandings occurring. There is enough for people to be legitimately upset about at this time without creating upset based on unfounded negative assumptions.

9. Don't ignore bonkers behaviour. If someone's emotions are resulting in behaviour which is not helpful, have a word. They may not want to discuss, they may get defensive, but it is best if you are at least able to explain how their actions are coming across to others. They may not care if there is an adverse effect on hospital staff, they may not care a jot about how you are affected, but they should be concerned if they are having a detrimental effect on their loved one. If they are not – shame on them, they need a good slapping!

10. Don't hold grudges. If someone goes temporarily doolallay because of the stress of the situation, take it in your stride. If it is you that goes bonkers, forgive yourself, and don't forget to say sorry to those you have upset. You will laugh about this one day – hopefully!

Challenge Three

Sorting Out Life Outside of Hospital

What happened next?

"Hello, this is Dave Carter, the hospital Social Worker. I thought I'd just give you a ring to talk about nursing care for your Dad. There are only three nursing homes in this area so they are pretty difficult to get into. If your Dad has a house he will be expected to sell it to finance his care. I will be able to give you a list…"

Er, just hold on a minute – I think any decisions about how any care needed would be delivered are for some time in the future, once we know how far Dad will recover. This phone call came when Dad had only been in hospital for 2 weeks. At this point I was fully expecting him to recover sufficiently to return home. I mean, he hadn't even got to rehab yet!

Dave's well meaning phone call sent me into a panic. Why had he contacted me now? Did this mean that the hospital planned to discharge him in the near future with no time in rehab? Why was he only talking of nursing homes and not other forms of care? Would Dad have to sell his house – if so he would have nowhere to return to if he ever recovered enough to go home?

As it happens, this call prompted me to make it plain that our expectation was that Dad would spend a large chunk of time in rehab before any such plans could even be entertained. This served to clarify to the hospital a situation that I was not even aware was muddy. All Sarah's chunterings about sanctuary, of which I was at that time unaware, had given them the impression that we wanted Dad to be discharged into nursing care as soon as possible. Oh lordy!

Dad did get to rehab, but after the first week, despite progress, we were given the message that his progress wasn't sufficient enough, and that his time there would be short. They had their targets to meet. Dad needed 24 hour nursing care and so Sarah and I had the conversation about nursing care that Dave had tried to initiate 5 weeks earlier. Dad was in an unusual position in that there were several possible locations he could end up in. His home was in Newcastle. He had lived there for most of his life. His friends were there, his house was there. It was the natural place to be. But, and it was a big but, the downside was that there would be no-one to be on tap to sort lots of things out for him. Up until now Sarah and I had shared this equally. She lived in Cumbria, I lived in Manchester. So the other options were that Dad would stay in Cumbria or that he would come to Manchester.

I imagined that choosing the location would be fraught. I was keen that Dad should come to Manchester, he had been talking about moving there to be closer to me for the past couple of years and I thought it was only right and proper that he be with his family. I was feeling surprisingly maternal towards him. I wanted to look after him and to make him better. I assumed that Sarah was feeling similar things and would want him to be with her. And of course it was vital that Dad had a say in where he went, it was his life after all. I could see no easy way of making this decision and suggested that it should be influenced by the availability of the right nursing care. Sarah was very quiet. Interestingly, at no point did she actually say that she wanted him with her. She had regularly told me that she was the equivalent to his wife and thus should receive the benefits of this role. I did not dispute this, the current status of their relationship was unclear, but because of this claim I was half expecting her to say that she would return to Newcastle with him so that he could go home. This offer never came.

Wherever Dad went, I was sensitive to the fact that one of us would feel hurt and excluded, but comfort and confidence that he was in the best possible place could help greatly in coming to terms with the decision. I was keen that we should work together to make sure that we both felt involved. I thought it would be best if we both did some research into our local nursing homes and come out with a shortlist of three each. We could then arrange to visit them together, and come to a joint decision on the best. I think I was being totally rational but entirely naïve. Sarah wasn't interested in taking part in any of this. When I had done a bit of research and suggested that she come to stay for a couple of days so that we could do a joint reccie she sent me a very curt email stating that she did not wish to do this. She had no interest in seeing these places, she had no special skills in choosing the right one and I should do it by myself. That was me told!

Visiting the nursing homes alone was a depressing task. By now Dad had consistently said that he wanted to come to Manchester, Sarah had not given any indication of doing any research of her own, so it was likely that Dad would indeed come to Manchester. I had to get this right. I was desperate for information as to the factors I should be looking out for and printed off loads of lists from the internet. These were a useful starting point but really the things I wanted to assess were not on any of these lists. I wanted to be confident that Dad would not encounter any sort of abuse and that the staff/residents would be the sort of people Dad would get along with. Pretty impossible to assess on the basis of a half an hour visit. It's amazing how many of our really big decisions are made on scant information. I saw many places but there was always something not quite right with them. I was not going to encourage my Dad to live in a place where people just seemed to be waiting to die. Then quite by chance I saw an advert in the local paper of a place 10 minutes from our house which had not been thrown up by my internet search:

- More like a 5 star hotel
- Big gardens
- Physiotherapy and recreational therapy on site
- Coffee shop
- Hairdressers
- Tuck shop
- Boutique
- Arts and crafts
- Village layout and atmosphere with different levels of care available.

On my visit to Woodlands, what really impressed me were the happy, smiley, alert residents sitting out drinking coffee and playing games on the patio when

I arrived. It ticked all the boxes. Excellent assessment report, full complement of trained staff, large sunny bedrooms which could be personalised with things from home. It was expensive, but it was so much better than anything else I had seen.

Both Dad and Sarah seemed keen when I gave them the brochures, so now it was just a case of ensuring that we had the finance to support it. Sarah had obviously been preparing for this step for some time. She had somehow managed to extract from Dad's financial advisor a breakdown of all his investments, she had gone through his bank statements and had a list of his monthly incomings and outgoings, she had arranged for Dad to have an assessment to see if he was eligible for Attendance Allowance (even though Dave the social worker had told her point blank that this was means tested and he would not be awarded it – it's not and he was). I was surprised that she had not told me that she had been doing all this stuff behind the scenes, we spoke every day afterall, but I was really thankful she had done it, that I did not have to add this to my massive 'to do' list.

I did the calculations, Dad got a good pension, if we got rid of all the unnecessary outgoings, factored in extra money Dad was bound to get for Attendance Allowance, and added the nursing component of his care, he would only be about £100 shy each month. His investments could carry this for years and there would be absolutely no need to sell his house. This was important psychologically. Dad needed to see that if he started to recover some independence he could return home. Although I was not sure how it would work in practice, I also thought that even if independent living was permanently out of the question, there was no reason why we could not take Dad home for the weekend from time to time to let him see his friends and to go to the pub which had been his second home for so many years.

So it was agreed, Dad would come to Manchester and would move into Woodlands as soon as we could make the arrangements. Well, he had always joked that he would end up in a shed at the bottom of our garden. With Woodlands being only 10 minutes away this was a very fancy shed and we had a very big garden!

Making sense of it all

Getting to know what care options there are and what sources of support are available is a total nightmare for the uninitiated. It must be complex, even Dave the social worker, whose job it is to know about such things gave us a bum steer by confusing Carer's Allowance which is means tested with Attendance Allowance which isn't. What adds to the confusion is the jargon and the inconsistency in the way different people use different jargon for the same things. Some people talked about needing a District Nurse Assessment, others talked about a Continuing Care Assessment. These are in fact the same thing, they are used by the local NHS Primary Care Trust to determine someone's level of nursing need and thus how much they will contribute to the nursing fees.

The lack of good quality, simple information is a real

issue. Straight away it was assumed by the professionals that Dad would go into a nursing home and thus that is all they talked to me about. It would have been more useful if all of the various care options could have been described, along with the criteria needed for making them into viable options. Although it was clear to the professionals that options such as residential care or a care package at home were not going to work for Dad at present, it would have been really valuable to me to know about these. They probably thought that there was no point in discussing these, that it would only confuse the matter.

However, by not discussing the wider options it actually served to exacerbate confusion, as well as undermining the confidence I had that we had gone down the best possible route for Dad and thus allowing those nasty feelings of guilt to sneak into the proceedings. Dad naturally wanted to be at home, who wouldn't. He recognised that he couldn't go home to Newcastle where he would be on his own, but he may well have had secret expectations that he would be living with Alex and I in our home. I had certainly considered this but knew that we would not be able to cope with the level of care Dad needed. Didn't stop me feeling guilty about it though, was I shirking my responsibility? Was I being a bad daughter? Clear information, automatically given, about the care options would make it so much easier for both the carer and the loved one to see exactly what, and more importantly, what was not a possibility. It would also give them something to strive for in the continuing recovery, knowing that if the goal was returning home the key things to work on would be more independence in X,Y and Z.

Ten top tips

1. First and foremost, don't rush into decisions just because you fear hospital discharge is imminent. They will not throw your loved one out onto the streets until there is somewhere with the care they need ready for them. Think of the field day the local press would have! Everything grinds very slowly, so long as you are actively looking you should not get any pressure.

2. Don't feel guilty if you don't want to/cannot care for your loved one at home. This is not always the best for them, it is not always the best for you. It is much better for someone to get professional, relaxed care and to see you everyday as someone who brings joy into their life, than it is for them to get amateur, frustrated care from their loved ones who cannot disguise their feelings of martyrdom.

3. Make sure that you discuss all the potential care options before making your decision. This means even the unsuitable options. Things change, a spurt of recovery can make previously unviable choices a possibility, changes in funding structures can make a difference to what is available locally. Health and social care is political – take advantage of any flavours of the month or vote catching tactics to get the very best for your loved one.

4. Find out about and apply for any sources of funding you hear about. This is a complex area and even the professionals can be wrong or confused. Even if you have been told you won't get it, apply for it anyway. The worst is that you get nothing ... apart from the satisfaction of leaving no stone unturned that is. Care is fiendishly expensive, and if your loved one is having to find a substantial amount to pay for this, they will need all the money they can get.

5. Make sure that your loved one is fully informed of everything you are doing and has a say, a big say, in what happens. Just because they now cannot look after themselves does not make their viewpoint less important. Remember, it's them who will have to live with the fruits of the decisions.

6. It is likely that different stakeholders will have different views about the best place of care for their loved one. Some will have more of a say than others. It is best if all stakeholders could work together and arrive at decisions, based on relevant and transparent criteria that all agree with and support. This avoids all that lovely sniping afterwards and increases the confidence of the primary decision maker that they have done the right thing.

7. When looking for residential or nursing care

it is natural to ask the professionals, those who deal with the various homes on a regular basis, for their recommendations. Be warned, you will never get any useful assessment or recommendation from them. Of course they know the good ones and the ones that are abysmal – but they will never tell you. They can't afford to be seen to slag off a particular place, or have a lovefest for another. Questions would be asked!

8. Don't expect to find a perfect place – they don't exist. All places will have pros and they will all have cons. In making the choice these have to be prioritised and balanced and the best possible decision made on the basis of the available information. Don't be tempted to bury your head in the sand and pretend that the cons don't exist. Knowing about them is good, you can keep a watching eye on these aspects and try to work out ways to minimise or counteract their effects.

9. All forms of residential care are expensive and currently people end up having to sell their houses to pay for it. Try to resist this for as long as possible, it can be highly motivating for some to work towards the goal of returning home.

10. Remember, any form of residential care is not a prison. Even the most disabled of people can get out and about with the

appropriate help. And if the worst comes to the worst and they hate their new home, or you have serious concerns about some aspects, they do not have to stay there. There will be others that do offer the care/atmosphere you are seeking. Honestly.

Challenge Four

Keeping that Face Smiling

Mr. Grumpy's story

Now then, Dad was never known for his happy, smiley, demeanour before he had his stroke, so heavens knows why I was expecting him to magically gain a sunny disposition now he was severely disabled and experiencing regular pain!

Whilst in hospital, as part of his menagerie of symptoms, he had been diagnosed with mild depression. This showed itself by constant drowsiness, a reactive monosyllabic style of communication despite strong evidence that Dad's language skills had not been affected, and a lack of any positive push to get better. All very reasonable under the circumstances, Dad was grieving for his lost life. At 79 he could not muster up any enthusiasm for the future, he was naturally feeling very sorry for himself. When he moved to rehab, I was hopeful that some sessions with a psychologist would help him come to terms with this massive and unwanted change in his life and that his frame of mind to tackle the months ahead would become more positive. So it came as a bit of a surprise to discover that the hospital did not have any psychologists, in fact I was told that there were no hospital based psychologists in the whole of Cumbria! So the only help Dad got to deal with his depression were a handful of anti-depressants. These did nothing to alleviate Dad's symptoms, which actually were relatively mild, and of course did not do anything at all to tackle the root causes.

On moving to Woodlands I decided that it would now become my life's work to help Dad to smile again. I initially toyed with trying to get him some counselling, but felt that his non-communication would make any counsellor's job nigh impossible. It's not magic! No, I would work on trying to spark some interest in anything, anything at all, and once that was in place I would revisit the idea of talking therapies.

Was this a mistake?

I don't know. I was mindful that it was unlikely that Dad would be an NHS priority for these services bearing in mind the well publicised national shortages, particularly as he wasn't displaying severe symptoms of distress. So it was likely that Dad would have to see someone privately. Looking after his finances for him I was aware that although he was not poor, paying nursing fees whilst keeping his home going would put a massive strain on his purse. So I thought that I would concentrate on getting the no/low cost things in place first, the things that have a real impact on quality of life. Baby steps.

Dad had a lovely large airy room at Woodlands. Lindsey, one of the nurses, had hunter-gathered him a little fridge when one of the other residents had 'moved on'. We set about making his room into a home from home. Key pieces of artwork from his house, long held dust gatherers, his music system and CDs, favourite books, games etc all appeared overnight. We set him up a little bar so that he could serve up drinks and snacks to anyone who came to party in his room. This was a good move. The Care Assistants, who were all about her! It was at this point that I decided to do a weekly update on Dad's progress and to email it to any interested parties. Not only would this keep everyone up to date but it would also be very cathartic for me.

True friends emerged from surprising places. Barbara, Dad's stroke worker from the hospital, started to send him regular cards and letters which were very motivational. She combined empathy, interest and a positive, humourous style. She was on my weekly update list and we started to build a highly supportive relationship. Barbara would sometimes come to Manchester for work and whenever she could she would pop in to see Dad for an hour. He looked forward to her visits and always seemed to be much more communicative with her. They did him good.

The other thing I worked on was getting Dad to get more involved in activities. This was more difficult than you could imagine. A previous TV addict, Dad would no longer watch the telly. He couldn't concentrate on reading, his memory problems made favourite games such as chess and bridge difficult. Then Alex hit on something. Dad's long term memory for factual information was pretty good. He could even remember trivia such as the name of the horse in Steptoe and Son! So pub quizzes it would be.

On his more talkative days Dad and I would discuss what we could do to make life better. We collaborated in putting together an action plan of things to do. We displayed this on his month by month calendar and ticked things off as and when we did them. Did it help

Dad? I reckon so. About six months after his stroke reports were given by Lindsay that Dad had been seen smiling in his sleep! It took another three months for this phenomenon to make it into the waking hours. The first time I saw one I wasn't sure what it was, but lo and behold it was a smile. A week later came a laugh and a week later Dad started making witty comments. No startling miracle recoveries, but amazing nonetheless.

Making sense of it all

Depression is a very common accompaniment to a stroke. From a layman's point of view, depression can be one of two sorts:

1. That big black cloud that descends out of the blue and is often down to a chemical imbalance in the brain
2. Feeling sad and hopeless because something very bad has happened.

When someone has a stroke the associated negative feelings are likely to stem from a heady mixture of both sorts. Something very bad has indeed happened, and in the execution of this someone's brain has literally been messed with. The chemicals may well be up the swannie. The handing out of anti-depressants like jelly babies is a necessary, but by no means sufficient way of managing depression. The pills can do wonders in sorting out the chemical stuff, getting people sufficiently out of the mire to get them into a position where they can take advantage of all the bits and bobs that get you smiling again.

Activity is key. It has always been my view that when people have too much time on their hands they can dwell on things too much. If life has taken a downturn this is not a good thing. That spiral of misery is never far away. However, when people are busy, when they have things to think about other than their own situation, that spiral is pushed out of sight. There is no time to be miserable! Unfortunately another delicious stroke accompaniment is bone aching tiredness. There's a double whammy, depression plus exhaustion does not auger well for a full and furious social calendar! As a carer you are constantly walking a tightrope trying to do the right thing. Your loved one may not feel like doing stuff, they may just want to sleep. That's OK some days ... but not everyday! Encouragement rather than railroading, firmness rather than fraughtness, finding things that are fun, enjoyable and easy helps. As with all things, start small and build up gradually.

Raising a smile is reward in itself. It can be a long hard slog before the first one comes. Don't give up, it will happen eventually, often when you least expect it. Dad's first came when his wayward can-can leg nearly kicked Chris, his physiotherapist in the face. Well, Dad always did like slapstick!

Ten top tips

1. Expect the depression, accept the pills initially, but don't rely on them to make things right.

2. If you get offered any psychologist input

whatsoever, bite their hand off. If, after leaving hospital you feel that your loved one would benefit from counselling to help them come to terms with what has happened, explore all the options including: NHS; specialist stroke groups; disability related groups; self-help groups etc.

3. Create a multifaceted weekly action plan with your loved one. Writing down the small stuff eg watch a comedy programme together, helps you to realise that you are doing useful stuff. All the little things really count in helping people to rediscover that life can be fun.

4. Find out what your loved one would like to do. Find out what motivates them and have loads of ideas yourself too. Try stuff out, and don't just rely on one sort of activity to get someone smiling again. If it doesn't work don't give up, try it again, and again, things do change from day to day.

5. Balance activity with rest and relaxation. Don't pack in too much at once. Spread it out so that there is always something to look forward to on a daily and weekly basis.

6. Don't forget the creature comforts. Well loved possessions from home, favourite morsels of food and drink, nice perfume/aftershave, fresh flowers, nice clothes all can play their part. Music too can

be very evocative, transporting people to relaxed and happy places in their minds.

7. Make it easy for friends to visit. Their gossip helps your loved one to reconnect with their old life. If friends are nervous of visiting alone why not come with them, or even throw a little tea/cocktail party to warm your loved one's room.

8. Keep friends and family up to date. A weekly/fortnightly email helps keep your loved one in their thoughts, helps them to reconnect with your loved one when visiting, reduces awkwardness, and actually is very therapeutic to do. Charting the various highs and lows as they occur helps you to realise just how far things have progressed, especially when recovery is slow.

9. Be a smiley role model. It is very hard for someone to feel positive and relaxed when those around them look fraught and grumpy.

10. Look after yourself. Do fun things and don't feel guilty. You are working hard, you need treats. It gives you something nice to talk to your loved one about. If they show any interest see if you can involve them too.

Challenge Five

Managing the Pain

When everything hurts

"I can't wear that shirt, the checks irritate my skin!"

A memorable quote from a man who has always been very delicate. Bless. Poor old Dad, everything did hurt.

When he had his stroke he managed to throw himself down the stairs, not only causing battering and bruising, but also exacerbating a previous back injury. The stroke had left Dad with a very poor posture. Although he could sit upright, as he got tired he had a tendency to slump to the side with his head virtually at right angles to his body. He loved to wriggle down in the chair but couldn't then wriggle back up again when this position became uncomfortable. You can imagine that all of this in combination did nothing to help his hurty back. As time went on Dad's left leg started to contract fairly dramatically causing him a lot of pain and making it even harder for him to stay sitting upright in a chair. His neck hurt, his back hurt, his leg hurt, he was in a bad way.

On moving to Woodlands I had high hopes that the two in-house physiotherapists would be able to get Dad sitting better and over time should be able to get a bit of movement in those lazy limbs of his. A better posture, combined with stronger, more mobile limbs, should in theory reduce Dad's pain levels which would in turn allow him to have a more positive frame of mind in tackling the world. Simple.

Unfortunately not so simple. The physios felt that they couldn't help Dad and that the natural pain of having physiotherapy would not justify the limited gains that could be made. What is it with physiotherapists – this was the second lot who felt that Dad was a lost cause – don't they want a challenge? This hit me very hard, Dad was now constantly asking me to 'fix' him, I knew that the boost of having a professional working with him on a regular basis would help reinforce ideas that if he worked hard he could improve. Even if little could be gained physically, surely the psychological gains would be worthwhile?

I recognised that doing nothing was not an option. If Dad felt that nothing more could be done he would just give up and sink into the abyss. I asked the physios if they would be upset if I asked a specialist neurological physiotherapist to have a go. They said they fully understood, they even said that they would do likewise if it was their father. And so it was that Chris Brown came into Dad's life.

Having Chris come once a week provided much more than mere physiotherapy. Dad had always been a man's man. What purgatory it must have been being almost entirely surrounded by women! The nursing staff were all women, the majority of the carers were women, the other residents at Woodlands were mainly women, and apart from Alex, his key visitors, Sarah, Barbara and myself were all of the female persuasion. Chris provided some much appreciated male company. Chris was also a welcome source of support for me. He was able to inject new ideas as to how Dad's myriad of problems could be tackled. It was refreshing to have a relationship with a professional that was not mitigated by unspoken agendas and budgets, someone who was willing to help me challenge the status quo as to how things were done.

Soon Chris's physiotherapy sessions were supplemented by a weekly massage from Zara and regular shiatsu therapy from Sally. Each of these sessions played their part in ensuring that Dad's pain did not get any worse, and despite sometimes complaining that each and every one of them were trying to kill him, Dad looked forward to these weekly encounters. He loved the attention!

Unfortunately no miracles occurred, the sources of Dad's pain were too complex to be magicked away by the laying on of hands. Thus started a seemingly never ending quest to help Dad become pain free.

A request to the GP to review Dad's pain management drugs resulted in a small increase in dosage which needed to be balanced with the increase in drowsiness this would involve.

Food supplements were added to Dad's diet to ensure that his spasms were not exacerbated by a lack of magnesium.

Chris started a campaign to get the GP to refer Dad to a specialist for botox injections with the view of relaxing some of those contracted muscles.

This all ground very slowly and almost a year later we were still waiting for some form of response.

Tens therapy was investigated but we drew a blank in finding any local practitioners.

Six months after arriving at Woodlands Dad still only had a very basic transport wheelchair with a pressure relieving cushion. Dad was spending more and more time in this. The staff had tried him in a range of fancy armchairs built for people with similar needs to himself. He had hated all of them and managed to squirm his way out of them on several occasions. Frightened that he would permanently hurt himself he now spent the majority of his time in his wheelchair. He looked a sorry state in this – it was too small for him, his legs dragged along the ground and often got caught underneath. The seat was too wide and he managed to curl into the most unusual and uncomfortable positions on this. There was no support for his head and he spent 90% of the time holding his neck, asking continuously for the carers to rub it for him. Chris suggested that we get Dad a fancy new wheelchair all of his own. As nothing seemed to be forthcoming via the local NHS wheelchair services we were up for it.

We went shopping, trying out all sorts of contraptions with Chris in tow. We ended up ordering a fully flexible, tilt-in-space model, the beauty of this being that when Dad's neck started to hurt we could tip the seating back to ensure good support for his poor old head. It had all the bells and whistles to help Dad maintain a better posture, surely a major break though had been made?

Well, despite now only holding his head for 20% of the

time, and having been the key decision maker in its purchase, Dad disliked it intensely. What can you do? We had set it up to help him maintain a reasonable sitting position, but he found this too restrictive. He wanted to wriggle, he felt like he was in prison! So we loosened it all up a bit to allow Dad more squirming room. And squirm he did. Why is nothing straightforward?

Three months after Dad had returned his NHS wheelchair from whence it came he received a visit from the newly appointed wheelchair specialist at our local NHS wheelchair services. It was clear to her that solutions still needed to be found to make Dad more comfy. She agreed with Chris that botox injections would be useful (ah yes, remember them) and that Dad would benefit from a wheelchair moulded specifically to his body shape. We were put on the waiting list!

Making sense of it all

Pain is personal. Understanding another person's pain is very difficult, our frame of reference is usually ourselves – how we would feel in a similar situation. But as we all have different pain thresholds and different coping strategies, we can experience similar painful experiences in very different ways to each other. It can be difficult to know when someone is feeling pain, when the feelings are more of discomfort and when they are simply attention seeking. The signals given may be indistinguishable from each other.

Poor Dad, with his contractions, his cramps, his reduced ability to change position, his dodgy back, it was clear that pain was definitely on the menu. However he also would howl that people were trying to kill him when their skirts gently brushed his legs or that he was in agony when the odd spot of rain fell on his head. He's delicate remember!

When Dad first moved to Woodlands he used to complain vociferously that the staff were sadists, that they were too rough, that they hurt him. At first I was very concerned. I was worried that he could be being abused – you hear these stories in the papers. I had many conversations with him trying to find out what exactly had been done and by whom. But Dad could never give any specifics so I just kept a watching eye on things. It wasn't until I started to have a more hands on role in his care, and he whinged at me too when I was trying my best to be ever so gentle that I fully understood the difficulties in assessing his pain.

For those who work with people's pain on a daily basis these difficulties do not disappear just because they are a professional. Holding a qualification or doing a particular type of job does not give someone any magical powers. Pain assessment is difficult and thus pain management is equally difficult. It can be extremely complex to pinpoint the exact cause, its severity and thus the best way to ameliorate it.

That Dad's pain was not sorted out quickly was a concern but at the same time this was totally understandable. It was more frustrating that there seemed to be no-one who was overseeing the situation and who had responsibility for Dad's pain management. Everyone did their job perfectly well, but everything was piecemeal and reactive. If Dad complained more the nurses would ask the GP to have a look. The GP would prescribe more painkillers for a short term fix – these would either work or they wouldn't – and he would happily get back involved if asked. Chris, Zara and Sally would do their stuff and make useful suggestions. We'd give them a go. But there was no clear diagnosis, no real plan, no-one pushing things along. I felt that it was all down to me to make things happen. But I didn't know what to do, or what was available, or even how to approach it, I was a concerned relative not a healthcare professional. It was very lonely. Just having Chris on board made a real difference. He was willing to get involved.

Ten top tips

1. It is hard to tell how much pain someone is in. Some people will play down agonising, excruciating pain, others will scream and shout about having their socks put on as they can get a slight tickle on their feet. Sometimes the same person may do both of these in the same day!

2. Pain is in the nerves of the experiencer. A firm grasp of the arm may not register with you but may be very unpleasant indeed for someone else.

3. Painkillers have their place but they are by

no means the only weapons in the armoury in combating pain. Unfortunately these may be the only weapons you are offered.

4.   Don't expect miracles. If the sources of pain are complex it is unlikely that the first thing tried to ease this will be all that you need. Be ready for a journey.

5.   Be willing to try a range of things, don't just rely on a cocktail of analgesics to sort things out. A recent report stated that it was a scandal that many older people lived with unnecessary pain. Pain that could be relieved via greater access to physiotherapy and chiropody.

6.   Unless you are really lucky there will be no-one overseeing your loved one's pain management. The GP will be sympathetic but they are often reactive, dealing with symptoms as best they can but not necessarily getting to the root causes.

7.   If the pain continues this is unacceptable. Don't accept it. Push to see a specialist. Keep pushing, this may take time.

8.   If things are taking an age and if you have the money, see what you can get outside of the NHS. Dad's wheelchair was far from perfect but it was a 100 times better than what he had been provided with. There is a lot of second hand mobility equipment available – it doesn't have to cost a lot.

9. Make allies. If you can get a healthcare professional to get involved and to help fight your battles the stronger you will feel and the more stamina you will have to get access to these limited resources. The more allies the better.

10. Don't forget the everyday remedies of pain relief. A few whiskies in the evening can go a very long way!

Challenge Six

Getting Out and About

On the road again

"Your father is terrified about the forthcoming journey to Manchester, he may not survive the experience. I am willing to accompany him in the ambulance if necessary."

Hmmnn, had I missed something? Dad had been in hospital for 3 months, he was now being discharged to come and live at Woodlands. Although severely disabled, his health was stable, what was all this angst about dropping dead in the ambulance? Was there something I did not know? Dad was now used to sitting in the chair for a few hours, what was the difference between this and sitting, or even lying, in an ambulance for a couple of hours? I decided that it was just Sarah being over dramatic as usual.

I knew that Dad would be anxious about the future, he had got used to the hospital, he felt safe. Now he was going to live in a place he had not even seen, with people he did not know. He didn't know if he would ever see his home again, he didn't know if Sarah would stay in his life – you bet he was scared. I took Sarah up on her offer to travel with Dad, it would be nice for him and it would be good for her to see Woodlands and to be reassured that he was in a good place.

As the ambulance pulled into Woodlands I was there with the official welcoming committee, cup of tea in hand. I was relieved to see that Dad had in fact survived the M6, but mysteriously Sarah hadn't. She was nowhere to be seen! Apparently she had changed her mind at the last minute. Over the next couple of weeks Dad took his time getting used to his new surroundings. Lovely though Woodlands was, I didn't want Dad to turn into that dreaded stereotypical care home resident who just sits in front of the telly all day. He needed to get out and about. If he could sit in front of the telly he could sit in the front of our car, he could come round to ours for lunch and even sit in front of our telly. So I elicited the help of the Woodlands staff in making sure that Dad was able to get out and about.

Alex and I had our lesson from Imogen, the Sister in Charge, on how to transfer Dad from wheelchair to car and vice versa. We had a dry run, working out how to dismantle his wheelchair and get it into our boot and then we were ready to go live. The first time we brought Dad round to ours for Sunday lunch we had an audience of staff out on the patio making sure that we did not manhandle Dad too badly and more importantly, did not drop him or bash his head on the car. It went off without a hitch, we even got a round of applause as we drove off home to a celebration lunch.

Over the next 3 months Alex and I got into the habit of bringing Dad out for lunch every other weekend. The more we did it the niftier we got with all this transferring lark. We were getting a bit too cocky so fate, and the weather had to get involved. On one particular Sunday it was spitting with rain as we picked Dad up. 10 minutes later when we arrived at our house these spit spots had mutated into a torrential downpour. Getting Dad out of the car was horrendous.

Alex pulled a muscle in his back, Dad's leg got caught on something or other causing him lots of pain, the wheelchair got soaked as we put it back together, as did we all. But it was worse for Dad as he had to sit on this sodden wheelchair through lunch. We were all in a 'never again' mode by the end of the day. This got me thinking, was there an easier way?

I decided to give wheelchair accessible taxis a go. After 4 journeys I knew that these were not the long term answer. They were fiendishly expensive and they often took over an hour to arrive. But the plus was that as no manhandling was involved it became feasible that Dad and I could go out by ourselves midweek. And so it was that I decided that Dad should get himself a wheelchair accessible vehicle of his very own, one with a ramp that we could simple lower to get his wheelchair in. Within a couple of days I had found a specialist dealer only 30 minutes away. Alex thought I was totally mad, but humoured me by coming with me on a reccie at the weekend to see how much these second hand WAVs were. He was impressed. Getting Dad in and out would be so easy in one of these. The next weekend we hauled Dad into our car for the last time and went back to the garage for a number of test drives. We bought a green one for £8000, just like that. Within a fortnight of the soggy bottomed lunch Dad had become the proud owner of a Renault Kangoo. This was actually the most expensive car that Dad had ever bought, but it was well worth every penny.

Having the Kangoo opened up a range of possibilities. Dad's outings went from once a fortnight to a couple of times a week. It was easy on a sunny day to collect Dad and to go for a picnic in the park. On a dull day, shopping at the Trafford Centre had its attractions. Anything really to give Dad some interest and some stimulation.

The other vista that opened for us was that it now became feasible for us to take Dad back to Newcastle for a weekend. We could stay at his house, we could go to the local pub and he could see all his friends. It would be very stressful for us, Dad needed a lot of care, we did not have the equipment they had at Woodlands, but it would be worth it. The only thing I hadn't got sussed was how to deal with the more intimate aspects of his personal care. I had started to investigate agency help when Barbara came up with the most amazing offer. She suggested that she would come to Newcastle with us and do all the dressing and toileting stuff. It would be her belated Christmas present to Dad. This was unbelievably generous of her, she had only met Dad a few months previously, she had only met Alex and I once during Dad's hospital stay, she was willing to travel 100 miles to a village in the middle of nowhere (well, 15 minutes from Newcastle, but it was very rural) to spend a weekend with virtual strangers who could be axe murderers. We felt we knew each other as we had communicated regularly via email, but really we didn't. We grasped this offer with both hands.

A month before our first visit to Newcastle I was feeling very stressed, what if we couldn't cope with Dad, what if he falls, what if he becomes ill, what if the heating won't work, what if, what if, what if? So I did what I always do and went into super-preparation mode. I went up to Newcastle to clean the house, get the heating working, make the beds etc. I got Imogen and the Carers to give me a lesson on how to dress and undress Dad. I became familiar with his drugs and when they should be taken. I let his friends know we were coming and welcomed them to pop in. All this groundwork helped me to feel more confident that things would go well.

But there was something else that was worrying me. After Christmas Sarah had visited Dad, and on her visit she had clearly read a card from Barbara thanking him for the candles he had sent her as a gift. It seems she had then gone through all his correspondence in his top drawer, seen Barbara's inspirational cards, and got herself into a frenzy about nothing at all. For the past few weeks I had received a series of emails in which Sarah was obsessing about Barbara, attributing malevolent motives to her friendship with Dad. She accused her of: being unprofessional; stalking Dad; being after his money; confusing him etc etc. In addition Sarah claimed that she had become friendly with a colleague of Barbara's and that she was sharing her concerns with her. So not only was Sarah slagging Barbara off to me, she was also spreading slanderous and totally unfounded rumours about her in her workplace! I challenged her on all of this but she took no notice, and accused me of having no compassion and of allowing Barbara to take advantage of Dad for her own personal gain. Eh? The fact that Dad had spent a whole £10 on a token Christmas present for Barbara was eating away at Sarah like a shoal of piranhas!

I had told Sarah about the planned visit to Newcastle, but I decided not to tell her that Barbara would be coming with us to look after Dad. I just had visions of Sarah turning up uninvited and causing a scene. Something that we all could do without, especially Dad.

Despite all of this bubbling away in the background the trip to Newcastle went incredibly smoothly. We all got there safely despite the motorway jams and snow. The house was lovely and warm. Dad stayed up late, ate well and sipped whisky (something he had been off since his stroke). We went to the pub and met his friends. We went shopping in the Metro Centre. Nothing went wrong and Sarah didn't turn up. Barbara was marvellous, she looked after all the personal care issues with only a little help from me. She also offered to come again the next time we came. We all jumped at this suggestion and got a date in the diary for a couple of months later.

Making sense of it all

How much you can help someone get out and about is predominantly about a state of mind. Not theirs, yours.

My Dad was probably one of the most disabled residents in Woodlands, needing the most amount of care. He was totally paralysed on his left side with no movement whatsoever, and to complicate matters he had no desire to try to do things for himself, making his actual disability more severe than it needed to be.

As carers, Alex and I were total virgins. We had no experience to draw upon, we were not even parents and didn't even have the skills of dealing with children to transfer to this new and frightening world.

However Imogen, the Sister-in-Charge, told us that we were the only family that took their relative out and about on a regular basis. Although the other families with loved ones in nursing care at Woodlands were very attentive and visited regularly, routine excursions out for Dad's compatriots were virtually unheard of, even for those who could walk under their own steam.

Maybe it was because we knew nothing of the pitfalls that our basic assumption was that Dad's life should be as normal as possible. If he could do something in Woodlands, he could do it with us also. Our expectations were that everything was possible, that we only had to find a way to make it happen. Looking back, getting Dad in and out of our Ford Focus was difficult, but at the time we didn't realise it. It had been our only option, we could do it, what was the problem? Once we got the Kangoo life became so much easier. But if we had not started with the premise that it was good for Dad to do normal family things we would not even have discovered that there were such things as Wheelchair Accessible Vehicles, and that actually they were affordable, if not to buy, to hire for a weekend.

Perhaps another factor in how much families involve the person in care in their lives is how much responsibility they feel for looking after them. Obviously the fundamental care is provided by the care home and its staff, but looking after means so much more than ensuring someone is warm, fed, clean and well. It means providing interesting experiences and fun, enjoyable times. I felt very, very responsible. This stemmed from the reality that Dad had come into care 150 miles away from his home. Alex and I were his only regular visitors and thus it was up to us to ensure that he was entertained. Maybe if he had been somewhere he had lived for ever, with loads of acquaintances popping in for a chat, the responsibility would not have been so clear, and the need to get out and do stuff less pressing?

Interestingly, since Dad got his Kangoo, and as the other residents and their families witnessed us going out in all weathers, a plague of Kangoos and other such WAVs broke out at Woodlands. Did we start a craze?

Ten top tips

1. Getting out and about adds another dimension to someone's life. Fresh air, new experiences, even mundane activities like going to the supermarket are all stimulating. Who wants to stay in all the time dozing off in front of the telly, waiting to die (Dad's words)?

2. Going out for a drive won't kill your loved one, even in an ordinary car. It's possible to do it.

3. The easiest, short term option is to book a

wheelchair accessible taxi in advance. And as you are not driving you and your loved one could go and get drunk if you wanted to!

4. If you decide to use your own car there is a raft of equipment and removable adaptations to help get people in and out of the car, even the most disabled of people.

5. There is nothing magical about transferring someone from a wheelchair to a car – but there is a knack. A knack that can be learned. Get a Carer or Physiotherapist to show you how to do it.

6. Get a Blue Badge. These open up the wealth of accessible parking that is increasingly available. Beware, do not try to take advantage of this when your loved one is not with you.

7. Start small. A short trip to the shops or the park is sufficient. Take a friend with you, they will boost your self confidence and make it into an occasion.

8. If you decide to buy a wheelchair accessible vehicle, go to a specialist second hand dealer. Buying a newly adapted car or paying for a car to be adapted can be expensive. There are a lot of second hand WAVs on the market. If going down this route, don't dilly dally too long. Don't wait

forever for your loved one to make a miracle recovery or to be up and ready for trips out, make them start living now.

9.   Expect your loved one to be a bit scared. Dad hated his new car to begin with, he was scared of being so high up. Sell it to them, people pay good money to drive around in 4x4s just to be higher than the other road users. Once they get used to it it will be fine.

10.   Once you are all used to having short trips, longer trips are possible. Investigate the accessibility of help if you feel you need it. If you do not have a Barbara, maybe the PCT can help. Or someone from the Care Home might like to come along. Or it can be possible to get short term agency help.

Challenge Seven

Fending Off the Vultures

Things that come out of the woodwork

"I just thought that I'd give you a ring to let you know that Mrs. Burrows has rung my office several times. She is concerned that as you have registered the Enduring Power of Attorney you will now be able to sell your father's house and car, which she believes to be hers. I have told her I cannot discuss this with her due to client confidentiality and am now no longer taking her calls."

Oh my goodness, what was Sarah up to now? Why the devil did she think that I wanted to sell Dad's house when we had been through his finances so carefully and it was clear that he could afford to pay for his nursing care and keep his house until he was about 100 if we managed his finances prudently? Wasn't it me who had been adamant that Dad's house, my family home, be preserved for Dad to visit for as long as feasibly possible? Why was she hassling Dad's solicitor about this? And why on earth did she feel that Dad's house belonged to her – she had only lived there for a couple of years when they had first got together. Then she had moved out and moved away to be nearer to her grandchildren. This happened years ago, not last week! She had a perfectly lovely house of her own, why on earth did she feel she had a claim on Dad's house as well?

A few days later things became a little clearer. My Uncle Gordon rang. He and Elizabeth had received a disturbing letter from Sarah which was full of angst, most of which revolved around her concerns around imminent house sales and my control of Dad's finances. From what she had written I now started to see how her mind was working. She was not, as I had first thought, concerned about the effects that a potential house sale would have on Dad, oh no, it was all about the fact that he had apparently left the house to her in his Will, the Will that he had prepared when she had first moved in with him. This really upset me – surely a Will only comes into operation when someone is dead? My Dad was not dead, he was very much alive, grumpy but alive. Was that all that concerned her – the fact that he may get round to spending his own money on his own nursing care, robbing her of her dubious inheritance somewhere down the line?

Things were slowly falling into place. Registering the Enduring Power of Attorney had not been without its problems. Dad had been highly organised, about 10 years previously he had got the EPA document drawn up before he had embarked on a visit to India. Just in case he had said. This, along with other important documents and heirlooms, resided in his secure box at his bank. When it was clear that Dad was coming to Manchester and that I would be looking after his affairs I had asked Dad's solicitor to register the EPA. We tried to register my certified copy but the Court of Protection was not having any and requested the original from the bank box. These delays and bureaucracies were a regular discussion topic between Sarah and I, she was urging me to get things sorted as she was finding it a pain going to

Newcastle to pick up his mail. I needed to register the EPA to get the authorisation to have it automatically redirected to me. So I took a trip to Newcastle to sort things out.

The night before I had an appointment at the bank to remove the EPA from the box, I received a text from Sarah late in the evening, saying that the EPA was actually in my Dad's desk. No explanation as to how it had got there. I went straight to it and there it was sitting perky and proud atop his dominoes! This got me thinking. When Dad had left home all those months ago he could not have predicted that he would have a stroke. He hadn't put the EPA in his desk. How strange, how did it get there? Sarah had obviously gained access to Dad's bank box after his stroke and had removed the EPA. She had had it all this time and had not let on through all the conversations we had had about it. Strange indeed. At the time I just put it down to stress making her do odd things, but now with what had transpired I was not so sure.

It had taken 3 months since Dad's leaving hospital for me to be able to take full charge of his affairs. On gaining this, other worrying financial aspects started to emerge. I discovered that someone had taken out £1000 from his account on his cashpoint card during the last week he was in hospital. Sarah was the only person who had access to this. She had paid some bills for him, but I had receipts for those and she had been reimbursed, so it wasn't for those. Her birthday was around that time, perhaps it was a birthday present? He usually bought her a jumper!

I started to wonder why she had not told me about this, I discovered it from his bank statements.

I also found that she had got Dad to sign a standing order for £500 a month in her favour and that three monthly payments had gone out, again this was signed that last week in hospital before he moved to Woodlands. Now I really started to get concerned. Dad had been quite confused at that time and was not seriously thinking about anyone's needs but his own. He was not really in any state of mind to initiate this, it was unlikely to have been solely his idea. However he was fairly worried that she would leave him, perhaps that is why he signed it? Thinking back, at this time he had also offered to pay for Barbara's new conservatory. She did what most of us would do, thanked him nicely and told him not to be so silly, that she was his friend and didn't need lavish presents, that he needed his money for his own care!

Again, Sarah had never breathed a word about this new regular financial commitment, despite all our detailed conversations and analyses of his incomings and outgoings in sorting out how he would manage financially. Perhaps she thought that I wouldn't notice? I decided to ask Dad about the standing order. Afterall, it was his money and he could spend it how he wished, but he needed to realise that this added monthly expense would eat dramatically into his investments. Three months on he claimed no memory of this whatsoever and made it clear that it needed to be stopped!

When I asked Sarah what the standing order was for

she went very quiet. Eventually all she would say was that she had thought I would stop it. No explanation, no apology, no nothing. I pointed out to her that if this continued Dad's money would quickly run out. If this happened we would have to sell the house, and surely no-one wanted that. All she would say was "if he can't afford it he can't afford it". I was so gobsmacked I let her sidestep the real issue!

Throughout all of this I had kept Dad in the loop as to what was going on. I decided to be factual rather than sensational when I reported each piece of dodginess, I didn't want to collude with Sarah or protect her but I also didn't want to make Dad more miserable than he already was. One day Dad was in a very talkative mood. He asked me point blank if I got on with Sarah. I told him that I used to, but that I had found her behaviour very difficult since he had had his stroke. He asked what she had done and I listed everything. Although none of it was new to him, just hearing the list had an effect. I could almost hear his brain working, recognition dawned in his eyes. He kept repeating over and over again what a silly old fool he had been and that he wanted to see his solicitor to change his Will.

Changing the Will took time. Dad was still in and out of confusion. Some days he would be absolutely fine, on other days he mixed up what he had been dreaming about or had seen on the telly with reality. There was no rush, he was not about to drop dead. We spent another 3 months discussing what he wanted his new Will to look like. We did this slowly, talking about it only on the days that Dad was perky, lucid and talkative.

Only when we were clear and consistent in what Dad wanted did we get a solicitor involved. Once the new Will was drafted and signed it was as if a weight had been lifted off Dad's shoulders.

Making sense of it all

You hear about people who take advantage of others financially in the Sunday Scandal but you never in a million years expect that someone you know will be the victim of this or indeed the perpetrator. It is a shock, it knocks you off balance for a while, whilst you desperately try to think of alternative, more palatable explanations.

In my case I was not sure if anything technically unlawful had happened but it was clear that the moral compass was spinning wildly out of control. The total amnesia in 'forgetting' to mention such a massive new outgoing from Dad's bank account on Sarah's part was very telling. It was also clear that this regular payment did not sit comfortably with the EPA which required me to only spend Dad's money in his own best interests.

I started to wonder if Sarah's seeming obsession with Dad's money was down to her suffering financially since Dad's stroke. No doubt she had got used to him paying for everything when they went out, but she was not financially dependent on him in any way. They had not even met until she was retired, she had her occupational pension, her state pension, her divorce settlement from her fairly wealthy husband, her own very nice house and car. She was not starving!

In trying to work out how to deal with this I talked to many people and was shocked to find out that most had stories to tell of family members who had been taken advantage of. Not one story was of 'traditional' theft but all were easily covered by that broad and distasteful concept, financial abuse. Recognising this is not always as easy as it seems. As with all things, financial abusers inhabit the whole of the spectrum. There are those who are downright villains, they deliberately target their victim, worm their way into their trust and affections and systematically bleed them dry, moving on to a new victim when necessary. They think nothing of stealing anything they can get their hands on. At the other end there is the so called 'friend' who never puts their hand in their pocket, expecting that others will naturally pay for them, using psychological blackmail and the withdrawal of favours if outings and presents are not forthcoming. And of course there are all the many shades in between. It is difficult to know what is worse, downright theft, or pressurising someone to 'donate' their cash to your cause through manipulation and playing on psychological fears. Outright theft is cleaner.

Once I had finally cottoned on that Sarah's focus was more on Dad's money than on Dad's wellbeing I was in a quandary as to what to do about it. Part of me was very angry. How dare she, how very dare she! I wanted to scream and shout, I wanted to do her some serious damage, I wanted to report her to the police, I wanted to ban her from ever coming near my Dad again.

But I didn't. Why?

I was also mindful that distasteful as her actions were, Dad possibly still got something from her sporadic visits. I was also sure that in her own weird world Sarah felt totally justified in whatever she had done, that she felt she was somehow entitled to Dad's long saved and hard worked for finances. Afterall, when removing the EPA from the bank box she had not touched any of the jewellery that I had inherited from my Mum, so she clearly had some sort of a moral code. I had to think what was best for him. She'd been well paid, in the 3 months that Dad had been at Woodlands she had had £2,500 from his account, so now she needed to deliver. So long as she was not able to do any more damage there was no reason why Dad should be deprived of one of his few visitors.

There was also a bit of me that didn't want to give her the satisfaction of making me lose control. Sarah is a woman who lives by her emotions, it is the language she understands, it is her playground. I, on the other hand, am a stranger in the land of high emotion, rationality is my thing. Why should I meet her on her terms? I'll do it on my own terms, quietly, rationally, firmly. That'll confuse her.

Ten top tips

1. Financial abuse is surprisingly common and abusers come in all shapes and forms, the abuser does not necessarily wear a mask and carry a bag with swag written on it. They are most likely to be close friends or family members. This is scary.

2. A common tactic of financial abusers is to manipulate the victim, playing on their fears and insecurities, playing hot and cold, getting them to collaborate with their own abuse in a similar way that the victims of domestic violence collude with the abuser or victims of workplace bullying protect the harasser. The need to be alert is paramount.

3. Once discovered, remember that there are different options for dealing with it. You can confront in different ways, but confront you must. Sometimes it can serve your purpose better to ask questions and gain clarification in a non-judgemental way rather than barging in with a shedload of accusations.

4. You may not be able to recoup any 'gifts' already made. But you can take steps to prevent any more leakage of finances / cherished possessions.

5. If challenging, don't just rely on a verbal interchange. Put it in writing and keep copies. Financial abusers have no morals. They are likely to re-energise later and give it another go. If you ever have to get legal it really helps if there is some documentary evidence.

6. Share your findings with others. Don't inadvertently protect the abuser by keeping it all to yourself. They don't deserve your confidentiality, others need to be alerted

too. Just make sure that you are certain of your facts. If you stick to facts rather than interpretations and assumptions you will be on firm ground.

7.   Always let your loved one know what is happening. A calm, matter of fact style should reduce any unnecessary alarm, especially if you can let them know what you have done to protect their assets.

8.   Don't be surprised if your loved one clams up. They are likely to be feeling foolish and embarrassed, especially if they have signed things or have been led into doing something silly. Make it clear that it is their money and of course they can do what they want with it. But also make it clear that they should never be pressured by anyone to direct 'gifts' in any direction. Be supportive and sympathetic and show them that you are on their side.

9.   If your loved one wants to make a Will or change a Will ensure that a solicitor is involved at every stage. They will be able to advise on the best ways to ensure your loved ones wishes are adhered to and will be an added strength if the Will is ever challenged.

10. If you feel that there is someone within the family or close friends who is a money-grabber, someone who would challenge the

Will if it were not in their favour, or who may suddenly 'remember' various promises which cannot be proved or disproved, get the solicitor to be a co-executor. They will be able to deal with all of that aspect without getting personally involved.

Challenge Eight

Living with Self Doubts

Good days and bad days

"Let me go, let me go, let me go, I've had enough. Too much pain. Let me die. Help me, I don't want to live anymore, let me go."

Whenever Dad said these words an icy chill went through me, was he so miserable that he really wanted to die? Was I doing enough to help him? What more should I be doing? Would Dad be happier in Newcastle? Why hadn't I been more aggressive about chasing up the botox more quickly? I need to sort out his pain. I need to get a better wheelchair. I need to ..., I need to ..., I don't know what I am doing, I am totally out of my depth.

I couldn't believe that Dad had got himself into such a miserable state. Only a couple of days ago he had had a really good time. Christmas was just over a month away and so rather than coming round to ours for Sunday lunch, we all went pressie shopping at the Trafford Centre. I browsed the cosmetic counters while Dad and Alex did deals with each other as to which perfume each would buy for me. Dad saw some fancy boxed designer mugs that would be ideal for Chris, Zara and Sally. Even Alex found the ideal gift for one of his difficult to buy for friends. We all felt on a high having picked up some inventive and stylish presents, so to celebrate we went off for a late lunch in Rusholme, Manchester's curry mile. Dad had mentioned a few days earlier that he had never eaten there, he was having a good day so why not? We chose a big airy accessible restaurant that was not too crowded. Dad was in his element, it was like the old days with him advising on dishes and telling me that he would pay for the meal. He really got stuck into the finger food and probably ate the most I had seen him eat in one sitting since having his stroke. He was obviously enjoying himself, he refused to go back to Woodlands until he had had a kulfi for desert, despite his back aching! Back at Woodlands Dad regaled the staff with tales of the menu we had just had whilst they were getting him ready for bed. They were amazed at how talkative he was and how well he had done. Alex and I had gone home with a warm glow, confident that a corner had been turned.

As well as just having had a really successful outing, Dad also had lots of lovely things on the horizon to look forward to. Not only was his new fancy, specially moulded wheelchair ready for collection later that week, but also the botox consultant had finally come to see him. He was very hopeful that Dad's pain management could be improved and that botox would help with the spasms and the contractions. Result. Christmas was coming and I was certain that Dad was in a much better frame of mind to enjoy the festivities than he had been this time last year, the first Christmas after his stroke. We were planning a little drinks party together and he had been very involved in saying how he wanted it to run. In addition to all this, Barbara was coming to Manchester for a spot of Christmas shopping later in the week and she had written to tell Dad that she would be taking him out to lunch. He had a more vibrant social life than I did.

So when Dad descended into the miserable mire it really hit me. It was not the first time that Dad had spoken about giving up the fight. Each time he did this, it set off a whole raft of self doubts within me. Self doubts which were normally kept at bay by the hurly burly of our busy lives. Of course I knew rationally that Dad's dark moods would pass and that the really bad days would be as fleeting as the really good days, but this did not help much at the time. As ever this prompted a totally unsatisfactory semi-conversation with me asking Dad questions and him just clamming up.

"Dad, you don't really want to die do you?"

"Too much pain, let me die."

"But Dad, the consultant is going to do the botox. People in Cheshire pay good money for that. You're getting a Ferrari of a wheelchair which has been designed just for you. The NHS has just invested thousands of pounds for this because you are so special. Shall we give these a try? They will surely reduce your pain."

"Let me go."

"You're having a miserable moment aren't you? You're allowed, we all have bad days, you'll feel better tomorrow."

"Please, let me go."

"But Dad, I know you are disabled but your health is actually quite good. You're not about to die."

"Kill me, let me go."

"Dad, don't be silly. I love you, I don't want you to die. If I killed you I would have to go to jail. And I would be so sad, I would miss you so much. You are my Dad, you need to look after me ... and Alex now that his Dad has died. Come on, cheer up a bit."

(No response)

"Is there anything I can do to help you feel better?"

"Put me right."

"I wish I could Dad, I really wish that I could. Let's see how this new pain management regime goes, I think that it should really help. This Consultant is supposed to be the best you know."

(No response)

"Shall we watch a DVD for a bit? How about 'One foot in the grave', you like that Victor Meldrew don't you?"

"Ok"

"Come on, let's have some of your chocolates."

Whenever we had these exchanges I always felt so inadequate, I wished that there were some magic words I could say that would make it all right. If there were some, I didn't know them. Luckily for me Dad's truly miserable days were only sporadic. Most of the time he was grumpy and complaining but he had no real desire to give up the ghost – he was actually a little scared of dying and would regularly make me promise to 'stay with him and make sure that he didn't die'. Interspersed with his usual discontented days were some days of pure delight and happiness and others of despair and hopelessness. I could never predict when they would occur and they always took me off guard.

The next day Dad was back to what had become normal, not happy or sad, just a bit of a grouse. He was back to complaining that the staff were sadists because they made him have a shower three times a week. We got all his presents out of the cupboard, and together identified who he still had left to buy for. Dad was quite talkative that day. He had been thinking and had decided that he would get Gordon and Elizabeth tickets for a show. This was a fabulous idea, I would arrange it, they would be so surprised, this was the first time in over 40 years that Gordon's present from Dad would not be a bottle of whisky! We planned our next shopping trip for the following week and Dad went cheerfully in to lunch. I left feeling much better and was determined that we all would have an especially lovely time this Christmas.

When I got home I got my new diary out and pencilled in a few possible dates in January for the next visit to Newcastle. Everything would be alright.

Making sense of it all

I am lucky, I am not a person who is used to self doubts. I have never had a problem with self esteem and I am usually confident in my own judgements. I put this down to being rational and analytical in focus combined with a high degree of optimism. I tend to think things through, rarely jump to dodgy conclusions and have a basic belief that things will work out for the best. Of course there has been the odd occasion where I have been taken by surprise but I have rarely been proven disasterously wrong. I know that for some, self doubt and self criticism are constant friends, but to me they have been very distant acquaintances throughout my life. As I said, I'm lucky.

It thus came as a bit of a shock to find out how powerful these emotional saboteurs could be. For the first time in my life my whole mood became sensitive to, and partly dependent on, the mood of my Dad on my daily visits. When he was having a good day I felt so happy and hopeful for the future. Maybe this time it would last longer than just a day? Maybe Dad was on the road to recovery? Or, if not full physical recovery, being able to get more joy out of life? When he was miserable and wanted to die I felt guilty that I couldn't magic him better, guilty that he was here in Manchester with me when all his friends were in Newcastle, guilty that I had sometimes let things slip and not chased up some things, scared that he would give up and slip away, cross that he did not appreciate all that I was doing for him, even more guilty that I felt cross with him!

Being a relative novice in the realm of these negative emotions I thus had no tried and tested coping strategies to draw upon. So I did what came naturally. This consisted of three main strands:

- Getting emotional support
- Rationalising the situation
- Planning for the future.

Significant emotional support came from three of the people on my weekly email update list: Ruchira in India; Barry – a long time friend of my Dad's in Newcastle, and of course Barbara. The weekly updates had charted all the little successes, failures and frustrations over the 18 months that I had spent looking after Dad. Whenever we were having a particularly difficult time all three would respond in different but all highly supportive ways. Ruchira would be sympathetic, she was so good at reminding me of all the things that I was doing and stroking my bruised ego. Barry would cheer me up, reminding me how much Dad had always enjoyed complaining and how well we were doing. Barbara helped me regain perspective by being positive and assuring me that Dad's negative thoughts were very common in those that had strokes and that they would pass. Another excellent source of support was Imogen, the Sister-in-Charge. I would often have a good old gossip with her. When Dad was having a bad day she had the knack of perking up my spirits with stories of amusing things he had said and letting me know what a 'good daughter' I was.

Whenever I was in danger of beating myself up I also gave myself a talking to. I would write down all the things I had done and all the positives we had achieved. I would also write down all the things still to do. The list of pride was always much longer than the list of shame, helping me to realise on a rational level the progress that had been made. The writing down was key. It made it all become ordered and concrete rather than the muddy swirl of mixed thoughts that were going round in my brain.

The process of writing the two lists gave me the vigour to start tackling the outstanding issues with renewed impetus, kicking me out of any complacency that I had gradually slipped into. I found that sitting down with Dad, on his more communicative days, to create an action plan together was always much more satisfying than just doing it by myself. It gave him the opportunity to prioritise what needed to be done, for us to share ideas for moving forward on the list of shame, and for him to see what had already been achieved on the list of pride. We would write down our action plan and stick it on the wall by his bedside table. I would have things to do but so would he. His were limited by what he could do, but very important nonetheless eg socialising with the other residents by going to recreational therapy at least twice a week, ensuring that he ate at least two thirds of his dinner each day (he was still too thin), ensuring that he worked positively with Chris during physiotherapy sessions to ensure that he got the full benefit from them. In this way Dad reinforced in his own mind that he was taking an active part in his recovery and that although progress was slow, he was still progressing. All this helped to some extent to keep those bad days to a minimum.

Ten top tips

1. Your loved one will have bad days as well as good, it is not your fault, there is nothing

you can do to prevent these from happening. They are natural.

2. When your loved one has a bad day it is likely that you will suffer from self doubts, guilt and a whole bag of neuroses. You can suffer from this delicious cocktail even if your loved one is having a good day. Don't worry, it is natural, it is human. But do try not to wallow!

3. Don't be reticent about sharing your feelings with trusted friends. They can offer support, challenge and perspective and can be key in getting you to see the funny side.

4. Be selective. Don't bother sharing your feelings of self doubt with those that criticise and reinforce them. Be aware that family and some so-called friends are not always supportive. You know who the emotional terrorists are.

5. Kind words are nice but they are never enough by themselves. Employ your rational, logical side as well as your emotional one in counteracting these demons. List your achievements and successes and view these against the things that are still to be done. Don't be afraid to list inputs even if they have not yet borne fruit. You are doing loads of things that you may not even realise.

6. Capitalise on and use these feelings of self

doubt to tackle issues. Prioritise what has still to be done, you can't do everything all at once. Think of ideas for tackling these. Try to think of several options for each challenge, there is never just one way forward.

7. Work with your loved one to create a clear action plan to move forward on the priorities. Identify actions, however small, that you both can take. Follow the rules of good action planning by having clearly assigned discrete actions with timescales etc. Review progress on the action plan weekly or fortnightly to keep you both focussed.

8. Don't feel too bad if your guilt/self doubts have resulted in an uncharacteristic angry outburst at your loved one. When you have calmed down, apologise and explain how you were feeling. The odd flash of irritation can sometimes have beneficial effects in getting your loved one to recognise how much you are doing. You don't want a medal or anything but no-one likes to be taken for granted.

9. If your feelings of self doubt are a constant companion rather than an occasional visitor, think about getting some more targeted help on these. Deeper, long standing issues around self esteem and stress are probably at work and cannot be cured with a sticking plaster.

10. Always remember whenever it gets really bad that you did not cause your loved one's condition. They need care because life happened to them, it was not your fault, you are not responsible for their stroke/heart attack/car accident etc. You are part of the solution, not the problem. Everything you do for your loved one is a bonus. But you can't do everything. You are not a miracle worker!

Challenge Nine

Coping with Loss

3rd December 2007

Dad died.

Dad's death was a total shock, I took it very badly.

The day that I was going to take Dad to pick up his swish, custom made wheelchair I got a call from Imogen. She told me that Dad had picked up a sickness and diarrhoea bug that was going around and that it was best to postpone our outing till next week. The bug worked its way through Dad's system in a couple of days but he was left with a bit of a lung infection. It was likely that a touch of sick had gone down the wrong way and was festering a bit in his lungs. The GP had been called and prescribed antibiotics. I was not overly worried, this had happened a few times before and a couple of weeks of pills had usually sorted the problem out.

This time it didn't. The infection took hold and a week later I was accompanying Dad to hospital in an ambulance. The week that Dad was there was one of the worst of my life. The roller coaster of his stroke was a playground ride compared to this. On admission they said that Dad was severely dehydrated as well as having aspiration pneumonia. They planned to pump him full of strong antibiotics and liquids intravenously and that they would know more in three days time. A couple of days later things were looking very grim. Dad's kidneys were not working, his blood pressure was very low and he was generally very weak. The Consultant took me aside and told me to prepare for the worst, probably within 24 hours. In shock I had to call people letting them know the very poor prognosis. Sarah came, Ruchira started making plans to get here from India, I was so scared.

But then Dad started to rally. His kidneys sorted themselves out, his blood pressure got back to normal, he was more responsive, and they were very hopeful that after a couple more days of antibiotics he would be ready to return to Woodlands. The Consultant would be doing his rounds the next morning and so they would have a better idea of the discharge plan after that. My spirits soared. That night, for the first time since Dad had come into hospital I had a good night's sleep. The following morning I rang to see how he was. He'd had a comfy night and would be seeing the Consultant in half an hours time. I had an hour to spare before my lunchtime visit so I thought I would make a few calls and let people know the much more positive prognosis. As I was just getting ready to leave the house, checking that I had enough change for the hospital car park, I got a phonecall.

Dad had died just before the Consultant had got to him. He had just stopped breathing. They had not tried to revive him as there was a DNR (do not resucitate) on his file.

I couldn't believe it. I just couldn't believe it. He had been fine just before. They had said he was getting better. I had just rang Woodlands with the good news. How could this happen? What was this DNR? Who had put that there? It can't have been Dad, he wasn't talking, that was one of the things they were concerned about. He hadn't made a Living Will or anything. No-one had discussed this with me, I would never, ever have agreed to this, Dad's life was on the up with the botox and the new wheelchair. Surely they couldn't just decide willy nilly to stand by and watch someone die when potentially they could be saved? Who were they to decide the value of someone's life, they knew absolutely nothing about it. How dare they!

Alex came back from work straight away and we somehow got ourselves to the hospital. I was numb, in a daydream. When we got to see Dad, lying there so frail, still warm, the crying started.

The hospital was hopeless, when I requested a meeting with the doctor to explore what had happened they sent a junior doctor who had never even seen my Dad. She said that he had been very ill. She apologised that they had not followed their 'procedure' about the DNR, I should have been informed and she was not sure why this had not happened. Did I want to take things further? Not really. I was distraught, my Dad had just died after finally receiving a positive prognosis only a few hours previously. Anger, despair and hopelessness battled for supremacy within my emotions. The last thing I needed was the hassle of making a formal complaint. It wouldn't bring him back would it?

The next few days were awful. We couldn't start on any of the arrangements for the funeral as the coroner needed to approve the death certificate. We were in limbo. I couldn't stop crying. Anything and everything would set me off.

It took four days to get the death certificate. As soon as we got this I went into a whirlwind of activity. Dad's funeral was to be in Newcastle and everything had to be organised. I drove up to Newcastle to see the funeral directors who were fabulous. In one meeting we had arranged for Dad's body to be brought back, chosen the coffin, booked a double slot at the crematorium, decided on the wording for the death notice, chosen the flowers, booked the cars, decided on a humanist speaker at the funeral etc. Coming out of the funeral parlour I sat in the car park and got in touch with Ruchira and Sarah to let them know the arrangements so that they could start making their own plans.

Ruchira's response was warm and supportive, empathising with me on having to make the arrangements without her help and saying that she would get a flight from India in the next couple of days and we could then go to Newcastle and sort out all the details of the service and the party together.

Sarah's response was as I had come to expect. On hearing that the service would be at 10.30 the following Friday she said that 10.30 was inconvenient for her as she would have to leave home at 6.00 in the morning. She had a policy of not driving in the dark but luckily her daughter would come with her so she would be able to come after all. I told her about the service and asked if she would like to say a few words. She wasn't keen, I empathised, I wasn't going to speak either as I would be too busy crying my eyes out. I suggested she thought about some amusing stories about Dad and that she pass them on to me and we could get the celebrant to weave them into the service. She then asked about the flowers I had ordered. I told her that I had gone for a lovely display of red and white roses as red had always been Dad's favourite colour. Sarah seemed unexplicably put out by this and told me that Dad had always wanted pink roses at his funeral. Had he? He never said. Well, not to worry, she could do the pink roses and he could revel in both! Deary me, she couldn't resist taking a pop, even at times like these. I drove back to Manchester fuming.

The funeral was really fitting, Dad would have loved it – if you can love these things!

Sarah had not got back to me with any stories but we had managed to amass a good range of anecdotes from Dad's friends from the pub. Ruchira and I threw ours in too. We had chosen some atmospheric Indian meditative music and the celebrant had woven the stories into a very moving, humorous and personal tribute to Dad and his little foibles. People got up and spoke, it was lovely. There was a good turn out and as we chatted after the service I could see Sarah had a face like thunder. It dawned on me that although the celebrant had managed to mention some of the key people in Dad's life she had not mentioned Sarah. Oops!

Sarah chose not to come back with everyone to the house. Not that she said, she just didn't turn up.

Ruchira, Alex and I had made tons of food, all of Dad's favourite things. If anything, Dad would have enjoyed the wake even more than all the accolades at the funeral. He had always been a party animal and to see his friends all there for him, working their way through his collection of whisky, eating curry and scotch eggs, telling the stories that couldn't be told at the service, singing songs, having their weepy moments before reminiscing about Dad with warmth and true affection.

He was well loved, I hope he knew it.

Making sense of it all

My Dad's death was a total shock. It shouldn't have been, he was 79, he was very ill, he had few reserves left to battle with.

It seems that no matter how bad the prognosis, death is always a shock. Dad rallied a bit before he died, he fought hard, he was not yet ready to die. The official prognosis was more hopeful, and this gave me a high from which to plummet. My initial reaction was constant crying, this was so unlike me, I think people were worried. But after a couple of weeks, especially after the funeral, the crying stopped, just like that. This also worried people who expected a more gradual re-emergence from the pit of grief.

What added to my initial devastation was that maybe, just maybe, Dad could have been saved. When he went into respiratory failure no attempts were made to get him back. The fact that some Consultant had unilaterally plopped a DNR onto his file had prompted such inaction from the staff that it made sure that they got a bed back. I, on the other hand, had lost my Dad, my Dad that I loved, my Dad that I had weaved the last 18 months of my life around and invested so much energy in his wellbeing. Grief was the overwhelming emotion but it was accompanied by those close associates of anger and guilt. Anger at the hospital, that they had arrogantly decided that my Dad's life was not worth saving. Guilt about everything. I had not known about the DNR, I should have done, if only I had maybe Dad could have been saved? Should Dad have come into hospital earlier, should I have pushed for this? Perhaps if I had, the infection would not have taken hold so tightly and he would have recovered? Even stupid things that were of no consequence were sources of guilty feelings, I had been gassing on the phone to a friend at the exact moment of Dad's death. Perhaps the hospital had tried to get hold of me? Perhaps I could have been with him to hold his hand?

I was lucky, my guilt was short lived. Probably because in my case there was no secret unspoken relief that it was all over. Dad's disabilities had been severe but we were struggling on nicely thank you. Things were looking up, botox and new wheelchairs made the future full of hope. I had not had to contend with that dreadful situation where someone you love is suffering and lingering. The awful mix of emotions, willing them to live, yet hoping that they will die peacefully and quickly.

It sounds silly but I also think that I was knocked for six because I had, at the grand age of 47, become an orphan. When my Mum died 10 years previously I had been very upset but it had somehow been easier. Dad was taking charge of all the arrangements and I was focusing on looking after Dad, making sure that he was coping. With Dad's death I felt incredibly alone. My lifeline had gone. At the back of my head I had known that if anything terrible ever happened to me, my Dad would look after me. This comforting assumption had not evaporated just because Dad had had a bad stroke and needed looking after himself, but now that he was dead that safety net was gone forever. Despite having a lovely hubby and a wealth of true friends, I was flying solo.

Alex was marvellous and did everything that he could. Ruchira was so supportive. Friends, and even acquaintances, were generous with their kind thoughts, but for a short while I was in a limbo of despair, crying uncontrollably. All I could think about was how Dad had died, how frail he was, and how I should have been able to save him. These thoughts swirled round and round in my head.

Having to make all the arrangements for the funeral was a blessing. There was such a lot to do in such a short timescale that the activity made sure that I had less time to dwell on the manner of Dad's death. The nature of the funeral also helped. Having chosen a Humanist funeral the whole focus was on Dad and his life, the good times, his essence. Talking to people about this and pulling together the stories really helped me to shift my focus from Dad's death to Dad's life.

I also drew some comfort from the death certificate. At

the hospital, all they had said was that Dad had stopped breathing and that they had not tried to revive him. This was very upsetting. However, when the coroner released the death certificate 4 days later it indicated that Dad had had another 'cerebral-vascular accident'. It seems like Dad had had another stroke. How bad this had been no-one will know, but it was somehow comforting that if Dad had lived he may have been even more disabled. He was just about coping with his current disabilities, having some more heaped upon him would likely have made life unbearable for him. I started to just, maybe just, entertain the notion that not being revived by the hospital had been a blessing.

Ten top tips

1.   The death of someone you love is always a shock. No matter how ill they are, they are still alive ... and then suddenly they are not. Nothing can prepare you for this.

2.   You will grieve. Grief is a process, people grieve differently but they all grieve. You may experience a recipe of emotions during your grieving process. Common ingredients are: numbness, sadness, loss, fear, relief, guilt, anger, denial and finally acceptance. How you grieve will probably depend on the relative proportions of each.

3.   There is no timescale on grief. For some it is the short, sharp, shock, for others it can be

a never ending numbness. Neither is 'right' and neither is 'wrong', but if you find that you are still wrapped up in the grieving process after 2 years then think about getting some help from a specialist bereavement counsellor. You could be locked into a circle of grief that you need a shift of perspective to get out of.

4.   Don't be afraid to tell people what you need, they will be falling over themselves to help you, especially during the first few weeks of bereavement, but often don't know what to do. During my exhausting two weeks of crying I got Alex to take all the phone calls. People kept ringing to pass on their condolences and each time I answered it set me off again. I was shattered, I needed to stop crying and regain some equilibrium.

5.   Don't let others take over all the making of the funeral arrangements in their efforts to help. Not unless you really can't face it. Being mentally active can help tremendously in getting the bereaved to reconnect with life and can reduce the risk of getting overwhelmed by despair and depression.

6.   At some point your focus will shift from your loved one's death to your loved one's life. Don't be ashamed of smiling when you remember them, you are starting on the process of closure.

7. Support others who are grieving too. In helping others and focusing on their needs as well as (but not instead of) your own, can help you in coming to terms with your grief.

8. Try not to get consumed with guilt. You did not kill your loved one, you were not solely responsible for their care, you loved them and they knew that deep down even if it was never spoken, you were there for them, you cared for them, it was not your fault. Guilt is a normal part of grief. Recognise this, but wallowing in guilt helps no-one, if you find yourself doing this, get someone to give you a talking to. Tough love.

9. Do the things that help move you towards closure. Unfinished business and regret are master locksmiths, they love keeping you in that stadium of grief, going round and round in circles, but never reaching the finishing line. What prompts closure will differ for everyone. For some it is the act of saying goodbye either before someone dies or at the funeral. For others it could be the process of creating a memorial or endowment in celebration of someone's life. For other's it may be as simple as finding out exactly what led to someone's death. You will know when closure is starting to happen, it is getting to a stage when remembering the good times causes a smile rather than a tear.

10. Do not think that you have to cut all ties

with your loved one in order to move on. They were a key part of your life, you loved them, they will always be with you. You don't need to rush to send their clothes to the charity shop, closure is psychological not physical. Take your time. Your life will go on and your loved one would want you to be happy. Talk about them, talk to them, look at photos, cherish your memories – but don't make the rest of your life a memorial to them.

Challenge Ten

Tying Up Loose Ends

My story

Christmas came and went. I was surprisingly calm. Dad had bought most of his Christmas presents before he had died. I smiled as I wrapped them up and sent them on with just a photo of Dad as the tag and a brief message from me about how much Dad wanted them to have the gift. This helped. I was starting the very long process of tying up all those myriad of loose ends.

When Dad had made his latest Will he had named both myself and his Manchester solicitor as executors. I got in touch with him in early January to start the process of sorting out Dad's affairs. I thought it would be fairly speedy, after all I had been dealing with his finances for 18 months, he had no debts, I was on top of things, I would contact all the relevant people, how long could it take? Oh I was so naïve. It took about 6 months just to gather in all the valuations of Dad's assets. The solicitor only had two things to chase but they were the ones that seemed to take the time. Mine were all done and dusted in a month!

Early on I had asked about whether or not I should get in touch with the beneficiaries of Dad's Will to let them know that they were featured. He advised strongly against it. He explained that in his experience, once people know they are to benefit they start spending the money in their heads. They make plans that don't take account of the lengthy time it can take to get Probate, sell houses, pay Inheritance Tax etc before any money can be dispersed. He was concerned that they would start ringing him up to chase the money, and each phone call he would take would cost the Estate. So with this advice I became much more comfortable about my decision not to get in touch with Sarah unless she got in touch with me. I had heard nothing from her since her non-appearance at the wake, I had heard that she was blaming me for her not being mentioned by the Celebrant at the funeral. Mistakenly as it happens, but that has never stopped Sarah! In March Ruchira started to get anxious letters and texts from Sarah, concerning her lack of contact over Dad's Will. Sarah had rung his old solicitor in Newcastle and been told about the new Will's existence, but of course she was not aware of its contents. She was clearly concerned that she may not feature in the Will. Ruchira copied the letters to me and told me that she had decided not to reply, despite her ability to put Sarah out of her misery, having a copy of Dad's Will. Ruchira was still smarting over some of the offensive emails that Sarah had sent her over a year ago. This was pay back time. Poor Sarah, if she had only contacted me she would have got the information she craved. There's stubbornness for you!

The biggest thing to do was to sell Dad's house. In January several local people had approached me, asking to be contacted when we were in a position to sell. As we waited for Probate I had kept them updated as to the state of play. They were all still interested in June when the Probate finally came through so we decided to sell privately. One couple, who had wanted to move to the village for years, came up with a fair offer and suddenly things were moving very quickly.

Up until then I had been fairly relaxed about selling Dad's house, my family home for nearly 40 years, it would take ages, I would have plenty of time to get used to the idea. But once I had accepted the offer it came home to me that in a couple of months I would have to clear the house and say goodbye to it for ever. I would no longer have a reason to return to Newcastle, the place I still considered as 'home', despite living away for so long. This triggered another weepy phase, nothing as dramatic as those first couple of weeks after Dad died, more of a tendency to become welled up over anything slightly touching on the telly, or sometimes over nothing at all. I had been fine up until now, occasionally getting a bit choked when chatting about my Dad, but nothing overwhelming. I wasn't sure if this was delayed grief or simply just being a symptom of a lady's time of life!

Despite a few relatively small hiccups the sale went through at the end of September. It was now 10 months since Dad had died and I still had had no communication whatsoever from Sarah. I had planned to write to her when we got Probate, telling her of her inclusion in the Will, but she pre-empted me, sending her contact details to Dad's Manchester solicitor so that he had it on file for her inheritance. He was a bit surprised to receive her letter out of the blue, and guessed that she must have been stalking the Probate Registers to find out the contents of Dad's Will as soon as it became public knowledge. That would be the only way she had got his name and address. I was aware that earlier in the year she had been very concerned about collecting the few bits and pieces she had left in Dad's house, she had sent letters to Ruchira expressing imaginings that I would somehow secretly sell the house and all its contents, and that her valuables would be lost forever. She was laying claim to beds, TVs, washing machines, sideboards, the whole shebang! This was all very strange as Dad had had perfectly serviceable furnishings before she had moved in with him. She had moved out several years before he had his stroke and had set up home in the Lakes with beds, TVs, etc., but hey, if she wanted the one's in Dad's house too I didn't really mind. So I wrote telling her about the house sale and asking which pieces she felt were hers. I asked if she would also like to take any personal mementoes from the house, anything that had special significance from the time that she and Dad had spent together. After a few weeks she replied saying that she did not need her bits and pieces after all and the only keepsake she would like was my Dad's gold ring that he always wore for luck. As I packaged it up to send it to her I wished I could be sure that she would cherish it and keep it safe.

Clearing the house was strange. When I had gone to clear Dad's room at Woodlands after his funeral I had been very upset. People kept popping in with their condolences whilst I was packing up his stuff and I kept bursting into tears. The boxes were still languishing in our hall untouched 10 months on. With the house it was different, everything had to go. There was a week between the formal Exchange of Contracts and Completion. The buyers planned to do building work on the house and wanted it stripped bare, carpets and all. I had a week to sort it. I got a house clearance firm that appealed as they claimed to do every clearance for nearly zero cost, selling furniture on and giving the rest to charity shops. Dad had wanted his bits and bobs to go to charity and thus I felt this would be fitting. My job was straightforward, I would sort through everything, salvaging key personal items, packaging up stuff that I could take to the charity shops myself, and then letting the house clearance people do their magic. I hadn't bargained for Dad being such a hoarder! I found allsorts, even old accounts from 1967! I also had to rescue all of my Mum's personal items, Dad had her old nursing certificates, old photos, even old love letters. They were really touching and set off more crying, Dad certainly knew how to write a letter. There was so much, I had to be brutal, keeping only the key pieces. It took ages.

On clearance day I was relieved when the people arrived nice and early as promised. Oh dear, my relief was short lived. The two blokes did a reccie and came up with the cost of £815. Apparently there was no market for Dad's stuff. I had been stupid, I had believed all the flannel about zero cost and had not got a proper quote. They had us over a barrel, we had a day to clear the whole house before completion, I had to agree. They then went through the house like a tornado, crockery was thrown into a duvet cover and dragged to the van, giving little hope of charity shop salvage. When the van filled up, perfectly good furniture was broken up to fit it in. It was so upsetting, the disrespect for Dad's things was shameful. Alex saw the look on my face and decided it would be best to take me off for a couple of hours while they were clearing. On our return, the house that I had grown up in was just a shell. Seeing it like that with no furniture, no carpets, was quite liberating. It wasn't our house any more, it was the blank canvas for the buyers in which they would create a whole new house. It somehow made it easier, locking the door for the last time.

Once the house was sold we were on the final lap in winding up Dad's Estate. Having the solicitor as an executor had its advantages, he was able to sort out all the more complex aspects of the Will such as Dad's bequests to all the Woodlands' staff that had looked after him. He also made me feel secure that if for any reason Sarah kicked off, he would be the one dealing with it, not me. A year after Dad's death we were in a position to make some dispersements. As ever I heard absolutely nothing from Sarah, however, via Ruchira it was made clear that she was very happy with her lot. So thankfully that was that.

Ruchira and I had continued e-chatting weekly since Dad's death.

What had started as a weekly update on Dad's progress had developed into a proper, supportive, sisterly relationship. The trials and tribulations of the combination of Dad's illness and Sarah's doings had brought us together. And now Alex and I were finally taking up Ruchira and Rana's invitation to visit India, something that Dad had always wanted to happen. In a strange way his death had made it possible.

Making sense of it all

When someone close to you dies your life is changed forever and when you have been their carer, that change is red and raw. You have spent your time looking after them, intertwining your lives, sharing plans, building your hopes on the basis of their progress and potential recovery, that change is not just emotional, it is physical, it is real, it is tangible. There is literally a big gap left in your life, all the time that you used to spend looking after your loved one, time spent just making sure their affairs run smoothly is suddenly hanging around on street corners with nothing to do. This time needs to be put to good use or it can fall into bad company and possible delinquency. That brooding guilt monster is always lurking waiting to pounce.

Luckily there is an awful lot of sorting out to do, and although this may not be everyone's idea of a fun party, it can help enormously in filling that chasm. If you are like most people you won't have a clue what to do or how to go about things. Don't worry. At the beginning it can all seem pretty overwhelming, but actually there is a wealth of advice available that helps you to break it down into bite-sized chunks. When someone dies it appears that everyone connected with the mortality business has a leaflet to give you. We got one from the hospital, one from the Registrar when registering Dad's death, one from the funeral director, even the solicitor had one to hand out. Although each came from a slightly different viewpoint these leaflets were consistent in their advice and helped greatly.

The funeral is only the first step. After this is over, sorting out involves a host of differing things, even when someone's life has been relatively simple. There will always be some assets that need to be gathered in, a few debts to be paid, a lifetime's possessions to be sorted and distributed, and maybe some last wishes to be carried out. Where there is a Will, formal Executors will have been nominated, if there is no Will a more informal arrangement may have to be agreed by family members. If there are any complexities in someone's affairs it is wise to involve a neutral professional such as a solicitor. They will charge for their input but it could be well worth it. Let's face it, people tend to be a bit more reasonable/better behaved when having to put their point of view to a stranger! The old adage that bereavement can bring out the best and the worst in people holds true and there have been countless incidences of families squabbling over an old chest of drawers like vultures fighting over a little lamb. Even if you have great faith in your family's ability to negotiate calmly it can still be useful as a professional has a vested interest in pushing the decisions along. I know of one Estate that hasn't been fully settled even though it is over 30 years since the person died! Vague Wills, assets tied up in property that has sitting tenants and can't be sold, family feuds and mistrust, can all be part of the heady mix.

Being actively involved in the sorting out can help you come to terms with what has happened. That it seems to take at least a year, no matter how simple you feel things should be, is probably a blessing, even if somewhat frustrating at times!

The more involved you can be in the tying up of the loose ends, the more likely it will be that you move through the grieving process over time and can come out the other side strong and ready to continue with your life, looking forward to the future. The sorting out process is a gradual and gentle form of closure in that:

- It forces you to properly accept that your loved one is gone.
- It helps you to realise that they will never be forgotten.
- There is comfort in making real their wishes about their Estate.
- There is security in having a degree of control over what happens during this process.

In many cases the sorting out takes you beyond just the affairs of your loved one. When my Mum died I helped my Dad take her clothes to the charity shop, but he kept a lot of her bits and bobs in the house that they had shared together. Not in any worrying, shrine-like sort of way, but there was just no need to get rid of them, they were joint things. Although Sarah had removed a lot of the obvious signs of my Mum in her tenure at my Dad's house there was an awful lot that had been hidden away in cupboards. So when my Dad died, not only did I have to sort out his things, I had to sort out my Mum's things as well. And because of the terms of his Will I also had to sell the family home in order that his assets could be divided between the 3 key beneficiaries. It seemed a massive amount to do, bearing in mind that I had many balls to juggle in my life already.

Under these circumstances it can be very tempting to take the easy option, and when people approach you offering to ease your burden by being willing to take things (cars, TVs, jewellery, even houses) off your hands, just think on. Sometimes these offers are genuine, caring offerings of help, and sometimes they are opportunistic attempts to get something at a knock down price, taking advantage of the situation. Trouble is, it is hard to tell which is which. So don't get drawn into making decisions off the cuff. The seeming bureaucracy of getting proper valuations for Probate is actually there to protect you and the Estate from grasping fingers. Several people approached me with generous offers for Dad's house, in cash, no questions asked. This was really early doors, we hadn't even had the funeral, never mind a Probate Valuation! Amazingly when the valuation came in, despite being notoriously under the market valuation, it was £25,000 above the highest offer, and when the house was eventually sold it came in at £50,000 over these offers, despite a recession looming. Thank goodness for due process. Being a formal Executor helps you not to get drawn into agreeing to these tempting offers as the big decisions have to be agreed amongst the Executors. However, it is not failsafe. I should not have been as trusting as I was with the house clearance people, what was I thinking of, accepting their assurances of a 'no-cost' clearance over the phone when they hadn't even been round to size up the work. I offered them a visit round but they were reluctant to come, the warning bells should have been ringing, but it was just another task ticked off my big list.

Ten top tips

1.   Be as involved in tying up your loved one's Estate as you can be. It keeps you busy and

is a really good way to encourage a gentle closure of this chapter in your life.

2. Don't try to go it alone, get help from a neutral professional who has no axe to grind. They are paid to help you and to make the tying up as painless and easy as possible. Take advantage of their advice, they have done this sort of thing before. Chances are you haven't.

3. Expect it to take at least a year before any settlements can be made on your loved one's Estate. Expect this no matter how simple you believe their affairs to be, something unexpected always crops up.

4. If a solicitor is involved don't be surprised if their tasks take some time, much longer than yours. You are just one of several clients that they are looking after, whereas for you this may be a main focus of your life. If you get concerned over unusually long delays a nag or even an offer to ring up yourself can get things moving again.

5. Be wary, look out for people who are waiting to rip you off. Unfortunately helpful, smiling faces are occasionally out to take advantage even under the most sensitive of circumstances. Don't let your grief, or your laziness, or your desire to get things back to normal as quickly as possible blind you to under-handed practices.

6. Use due process to your advantage, but don't get into unnecessary formalities if you really don't need to. For example, it would be silly to verbally accept a cash offer on a house before it has been valued. However, if it has been valued and the offer is fair/good then there is no real need to engage an Estate Agent in an attempt to get a bidding war going and maybe a couple of hundred more. The costs outweigh the benefits.

7. Don't be surprised if the process of sorting out your loved one's things triggers another phase of grief. Grieving is a process, not a one-off event. It is common than an initial period of extreme grief is followed by months of calm before kicking off again. It is all part of the process, a process that moves you on to the next step.

8. Don't feel guilty about getting rid of your loved one's prized possessions. Keep some things, but you can't keep everything. Give away as much as you can to those who will appreciate it. You will have to throw out some personal stuff, letters, photos, school reports etc., it is only stuff, people keep all sorts and never look at it again. Just because your loved one was a hoarder doesn't mean that you have to be too.

9. Try to avoid needless family bun fights over bits and bobs. Some people may try to get more than their fair share and it is all too

easy to be drawn into squabbles over possessions that you really don't care about. Just because your family members are irritating you by being grasping and grabbing. Try to step back, if it really means so much to them, let them have it. That way, you can concentrate on the one or two things that do mean a lot to you. Your dignity for one.

10. And so to the hundredth top tip. Be proud of all your efforts, you were no expert but you tried your very best. And that is all any of us can do.

Epilogue

Life Is For Living

25th January 2009.

Weaving through the congested traffic of Kolkata at a ridiculous speed was both terrifying and exhilarating. Ruchira and Rana's driver was very skilful, judging to the millimetre the size of any emerging space that their People Carrier could fit into. As a space opened up on the dual carriageway it was immediately filled with cars, buses, cyclists, tuk-tuks, cows, camels or pedestrians. All life was here, intertwining in a seemingly chaotic way, whilst living in harmony together. Eventually we left the sprawling city and drove at speed on country roads towards the Ganges Delta where we were to pick up our boat to take us tiger spotting in the uninhabited mangrove swamps of the delta. The country roads were not quiet and barely a minute went past without us overtaking a cycle rickshaw carrying a family of 14 or swerving to avoid a herd of cattle that had decided to lay down in the road.

We travelled through miles of paddy fields interspersed with heaving villages all of whom seemed to be having a carnival where everyone was out on the streets. The colours, sounds and smells were bright and in your face. Vivid images of women dressed in beautiful evening dress style saris of oranges, yellows, pinks and turquoises digging leaves and muck out of the ditches mingled with exotic smells of spices and cow dung. All of this played out against a symphony of constantly tooting car horns and jingly jangly music.

On reaching the town where we were to pick up our boat we were totally surrounded by people wanting to have a good look at the Europeans. Ruchira and Rana were treating us like royalty, but this made us feel like celebrities, being swamped by the paparazzi. On getting out of the car people thronged around us trying to carry our bags, offering us souvenirs or just wanting their photographs taken with the foreigners. We clambered onto the boat that Rana had hired for our trip and as it chugged out of harbour he opened up his cool box and handed round the icy beers. Ruchira dipped into her bag and brought out some delicious homemade samosas. We sat there contented in the warm sun with the gentle river breeze on our faces and chatted fondly about Dad and how happy he would be if he could see us all together like this. As we got further into the depths of the mangroves the engines were cut and we revelled in the spooky landscape and the companionable silence. What was that rustling behind the ferns? Could it be a tiger watching us? Well, you never can tell!